Illumine My Family

Illumine My Family

Prayers and Meditations from the Bahá'í Faith

compiled by Bahá'í Publishing

Bahá'í
PUBLISHING
Wilmette, Illinois

Bahá'í Publishing
415 Linden Avenue, Wilmette, Illinois 60091-2844

12   11   10   09   4   3   2   1

Library of Congress Cataloging-in-Publication Data
Illumine my family : prayers and meditations from the
Baha'i faith / [compiled by Bahá'u'lláh, the Bab, and 'Abdu'l-
Bahá].
    p. cm.
  Includes bibliographical references and index.
  ISBN-13: 978-1-931847-62-9 (alk. paper)
  ISBN-10: 1-931847-62-2 (alk. paper)
  1. Bahai Faith—Prayers and devotions. I. Bahá'u'lláh,
1817–1892. II. Bab, 'Ali Muhammad Shirazi, 1819–1850. III.
'Abdu'l-Bahá, 1844–1921.

  BP360.I45 2009
  297.9'3433—dc22

                                          2008055056

Cover design by Misha Maynerick
Book design by Suni D. Hannan

Contents

Introduction

The family unit is given great importance in the writings of the Bahá'í Faith. Bahá'u'lláh, the Prophet and Founder of the Faith, describes marriage as "a fortress for well-being," and His great-grandson Shoghi Effendi, the Faith's Guardian, describes marriage and the family as "the bedrock of the whole structure of human society." The concept of unity is central to the teachings of the Faith, and the family unit is seen as the foundation on which this unity is built on a societal level.

The Bahá'í Faith is an independent world religion that began in 1844 in Persia (present-day Iran). Since its inception the Bahá'í Faith has spread to 235 nations and territories and has been accepted by more than five million people. Bahá'ís believe that there is only one God, that all the major world religions come from God, and that all the members of the human race are essentially members of one family. Bahá'ís strive to eliminate all forms of prejudice and believe that people of all races, nations, social status, and religious backgrounds are equal in the sight of God. The Bahá'í Faith also teaches that each individual is responsible for the independent investigation of truth, that science and religion are in harmony, and that men and women are equal in the sight of God.

The Bahá'í writings cover a vast range of topics and touch on virtually every aspect of life. The passages compiled in this book offer prayers and food for thought on subjects relevant to families regardless of their backgrounds. Subjects covered include marriage, parents, motherhood, children, love, the equality of women and men, healing, the loss of a loved one, and more. Included here are passages from the writings of Bahá'u'lláh; those of His forerunner, the Báb; and the writings and recorded utterances of Bahá'u'lláh's eldest son and successor, 'Abdu'l-Bahá. Each section of the book contains a selection of prayers followed by meditative passages relevant to the theme of the section. *Illumine My Family* has been prepared with the hope that it will assist families to grow together and to foster strong relationships with each other and with God.

According to the teachings of Bahá'u'lláh the family, being a human unit, must be educated according to the rules of sanctity. All the virtues must be taught the family. The integrity of the family bond must be constantly considered, and the rights of the individual members must not be transgressed. The rights of the son, the father, the mother—none of them must be transgressed, none of them must be arbitrary. Just as the son has certain obligations to his father, the father, likewise, has certain obligations to his son. The mother, the sister and other members of the household have their certain prerogatives. All these rights and prerogatives must be conserved, yet the unity of the family must be sustained. The injury of one shall be considered the injury of all; the comfort of each, the comfort of all; the honor of one, the honor of all.

—*'Abdu'l-Bahá*

❧ ❧ ❧

It is highly important for man to raise a family. So long as he is young, because of youthful self-complacency, he does not realize its significance, but this will be a source of regret when he grows old. . . . In this glorious Cause the life of a married couple should resemble the life of the angels in heaven—a life full of joy and spiritual delight, a life of unity and concord, a friendship both mental and physical. The home should be orderly and well-organized. Their ideas and thoughts should be like the rays of the sun of truth and the radiance of the brilliant stars in the heavens. Even as two birds they should warble melodies upon the branches of the tree of fellowship and harmony. They should always be elated with joy and gladness and be a source of happiness to the hearts of others. They should set an example to their fellowmen, manifest a true and sincere love towards each other and educate their children in such a manner as to blazon the fame and glory of their family.

—*'Abdu'l-Bahá*

Children

1

Praised be Thou, O Lord my God! Graciously grant that this infant be fed from the breast of Thy tender mercy and loving providence and be nourished with the fruit of Thy celestial trees. Suffer him not to be committed to the care of anyone save Thee, inasmuch as Thou, Thyself, through the potency of Thy sovereign will and power, didst create and call him into being. There is none other God but Thee, the Almighty, the All-Knowing.

Lauded art Thou, O my Best Beloved, waft over him the sweet savors of Thy transcendent bounty and the fragrances of Thy holy bestowals. Enable him then to seek shelter beneath the shadow of Thy most exalted Name, O Thou Who holdest in Thy grasp the kingdom of names and attributes. Verily, Thou art potent to do what Thou willest, and Thou art indeed the Mighty, the Exalted, the Ever-Forgiving, the Gracious, the Generous, the Merciful.

—*Bahá'u'lláh*

2

O Thou peerless Lord! Let this suckling babe be nursed from the breast of Thy loving-kindness, guard it within the cradle of Thy safety and protection and grant that it be reared in the arms of Thy tender affection.

—'Abdu'l-Bahá

3

O God! Rear this little babe in the bosom of Thy love, and give it milk from the breast of Thy Providence. Cultivate this fresh plant in the rose garden of Thy love and aid it to grow through the showers of Thy bounty. Make it a child of the kingdom, and lead it to Thy heavenly realm. Thou art powerful and kind, and Thou art the Bestower, the Generous, the Lord of surpassing bounty.

—'Abdu'l-Bahá

4

O God! Educate these children. These children are the plants of Thine orchard, the flowers of Thy meadow, the roses of Thy garden. Let Thy rain fall upon them; let the Sun of Reality shine upon them with Thy love. Let Thy breeze refresh them in order that they may be trained, grow and develop, and appear in the utmost beauty. Thou art the Giver. Thou art the Compassionate.

—*'Abdu'l-Bahá*

5

O Thou kind Lord! These lovely children are the handiwork of the fingers of Thy might and the wondrous signs of Thy greatness. O God! Protect these children, graciously assist them to be educated and enable them to render service to the world of humanity. O God! These children are pearls, cause them to be nurtured within the shell of Thy loving-kindness.

Thou art the Bountiful, the All-Loving.

—*'Abdu'l-Bahá*

6

O Lord! Make these children excellent plants. Let them grow and develop in the Garden of Thy Covenant, and bestow freshness and beauty through the outpourings of the clouds of the Abhá Kingdom.

O Thou kind Lord! I am a little child, exalt me by admitting me to the kingdom. I am earthly, make me heavenly; I am of the world below, let me belong to the realm above; gloomy, suffer me to become radiant; material, make me spiritual, and grant that I may manifest Thine infinite bounties.

Thou art the Powerful, the All-Loving.

—*'Abdu'l-Bahá*

7

O my Lord! O my Lord!
I am a child of tender years. Nourish me from the breast of Thy mercy, train me in the bosom of Thy love, educate me in the school of Thy guidance and develop me under the shadow of Thy bounty. Deliver me from darkness, make me a brilliant light; free me from unhappiness, make me a flower of the rose garden; suffer me to become a servant of Thy threshold and confer upon me the disposition and nature of the righteous; make me a cause of bounty to the human world, and crown my head with the diadem of eternal life.

Verily, Thou art the Powerful, the Mighty, the Seer, the Hearer.

—*'Abdu'l-Bahá*

8

O Peerless Lord! Be Thou a shelter for this poor child and a kind and forgiving Master unto this erring and unhappy soul. O Lord!

Though we are but worthless plants, yet we belong to Thy garden of roses. Though saplings without leaves and blossoms, yet we are a part of Thine orchard. Nurture this plant then through the outpourings of the clouds of Thy tender mercy and quicken and refresh this sapling through the reviving breath of Thy spiritual springtime. Suffer him to become heedful, discerning and noble, and grant that he may attain eternal life and abide in Thy Kingdom for evermore.

—*'Abdu'l-Bahá*

9

O Lord! Make this youth radiant, and confer Thy bounty upon this poor creature. Bestow upon him knowledge, grant him added strength at the break of every morn and guard him within the shelter of Thy protection so that he may be freed from error, may devote himself to the service of Thy Cause, may guide the wayward, lead the hapless, free the captives and awaken the heedless, that all may be blessed with Thy remembrance and praise. Thou art the Mighty and the Powerful.

—*'Abdu'l-Bahá*

৶ ৶ ৶

10

Among the greatest of all services that can possibly be rendered by man to Almighty God is the education and training of children, young plants of the Abhá Paradise,* so that these children, fostered by grace in the way of salvation, growing like pearls of divine bounty in the shell of education, will one day bejewel the crown of abiding glory.

It is, however, very difficult to undertake this service, even harder to succeed in it. I hope that thou wilt acquit thyself well in this most important of tasks, and successfully carry the day, and become an ensign of God's abounding grace; that these children, reared one and all in the holy Teachings, will develop natures like unto the sweet airs that blow across the gardens of the All-Glorious, and will waft their fragrance around the world.

—*'Abdu'l-Bahá*

11

Every day at first light, ye gather the . . . children together and teach them the communes and prayers. This is a most praiseworthy

---

* *The Most Glorious Paradise:* the spiritual world beyond this world.

act, and bringeth joy to the children's hearts: that they should, at every morn, turn their faces toward the Kingdom and make mention of the Lord and praise His Name, and in the sweetest of voices, chant and recite.

These children are even as young plants, and teaching them the prayers is as letting the rain pour down upon them, that they may wax tender and fresh, and the soft breezes of the love of God may blow over them, making them to tremble with joy.

Blessedness awaiteth you, and a fair haven.

—*'Abdu'l-Bahá*

12

It is incumbent upon the mothers to rear their little ones even as a gardener tendeth his young plants. Let them strive by day and by night to establish within their children faith and certitude, the fear of God, the love of the Beloved of the worlds, and all good qualities and traits.

—*'Abdu'l-Bahá*

Parents

I pray Thee, O my Lord, by Thy hidden, Thy treasured Name, that calleth aloud in the kingdom of creation, and summoneth all peoples to the Tree beyond which there is no passing, the seat of transcendent glory, to rain down upon us, and upon Thy servants, the overflowing rain of Thy mercy, that it may cleanse us from the remembrance of all else but Thee, and draw us nigh unto the shores of the ocean of Thy grace. Ordain, O Lord, through Thy most exalted Pen, that which will immortalize our souls in the Realm of glory, will perpetuate our names in Thy Kingdom, and safeguard our lives in the treasuries of Thy protection and our bodies in the stronghold of Thy inviolable fastness. Powerful art Thou over all things, be they of the past or of the future. No God is there but Thee, the omnipotent Protector, the Self-Subsisting.

Thou seest, O Lord, our suppliant hands lifted up towards the heaven of Thy favor and bounty. Grant that they may be filled with the treasures of Thy munificence and bountiful favor. Forgive us, and our fathers, and our mothers, and fulfill whatsoever we have desired from the ocean of

Thy grace and Divine generosity. Accept, O Beloved of our hearts, all our works in Thy path. Thou art, verily, the Most Powerful, the Most Exalted, the Incomparable, the One, the Forgiving, the Gracious.

—*Bahá'u'lláh*

2

O Lord! In this Most Great Dispensation Thou dost accept the intercession of children in behalf of their parents. This is one of the special infinite bestowals of this Dispensation. Therefore, O Thou kind Lord, accept the request of this Thy servant at the threshold of Thy singleness and submerge his father in the ocean of Thy grace, because this son hath arisen to render Thee service and is exerting effort at all times in the pathway of Thy love. Verily, Thou art the Giver, the Forgiver and the Kind!

—*'Abdu'l-Bahá*

❧ ❧ ❧

3

Say, O My people! Show honor to your parents and pay homage to them. This will cause blessings to descend upon you from the clouds of the bounty of your Lord, the Exalted, the Great.

—*Bahá'u'lláh*

4

The fruits of the tree of existence are trustworthiness, loyalty, truthfulness and purity. After the recognition of the oneness of the Lord, exalted be He, the most important of all duties is to have due regard for the rights of one's parents. This matter hath been mentioned in all the Books of God.

—*Bahá'u'lláh*

5

The fruits that best befit the tree of human life are trustworthiness and godliness, truthfulness and sincerity; but greater than all, after recognition of the unity of God, praised and glorified be He, is regard for the rights that are due to one's parents. This teaching hath been mentioned in all the Books of God, and reaffirmed by the Most Exalted Pen. Consider that which the Merciful Lord hath revealed in the Qur'án, exalted are His words: "Worship ye God, join with Him no peer or likeness; and show forth kindliness and charity towards your parents . . ." Observe how loving-kindness to one's parents hath been linked to recognition of the one true God! Happy they who are endued with true wisdom and understanding, who see and perceive, who read and understand, and who observe that which God hath revealed in the Holy Books of old, and in this incomparable and wondrous Tablet.

—*Bahá'u'lláh*

6

A father and mother endure the greatest troubles and hardships for their children; and often when the children have reached the age of maturity, the parents pass on to the other world. Rarely does it happen that a father and mother in this world see the reward of the care and trouble they have undergone for their children. Therefore, children, in return for this care and trouble, must show forth charity and beneficence, and must implore pardon and forgiveness for their parents. So you ought, in return for the love and kindness shown you by your father, to give to the poor for his sake, with greatest submission and humility implore pardon and remission of sins, and ask for the supreme mercy.

—*'Abdu'l-Bahá*

7

If thou wouldst show kindness and consideration to thy parents so that they may feel generally pleased, this would also please Me, for parents must be highly respected and it is essential that they should feel contented, provided they deter thee not from gaining access to the Threshold of the Almighty, nor keep thee back from walking in the way of the Kingdom. Indeed it behooveth them to encourage and spur thee on in this direction.

—'Abdu'l-Bahá

Parenting

Prayer for Expectant Mothers
1

My Lord! My Lord! I praise Thee and I thank Thee for that whereby Thou hast favored Thine humble maidservant, Thy slave beseeching and supplicating Thee, because Thou hast verily guided her unto Thine obvious Kingdom and caused her to hear Thine exalted Call in the contingent world and to behold Thy Signs which prove the appearance of Thy victorious reign over all things.

O my Lord, I dedicate that which is in my womb unto Thee. Then cause it to be a praiseworthy child in Thy Kingdom and a fortunate one by Thy favor and Thy generosity; to develop and to grow up under the charge of Thine education. Verily, Thou art the Gracious! Verily, Thou art the Lord of Great Favor!

—'Abdu'l-Bahá

෨ ෨ ෨

2

He that bringeth up his son or the son of another, it is as though he hath brought up a son of Mine.

—*Bahá'u'lláh*

3

Every child is potentially the light of the world—and at the same time its darkness; wherefore must the question of education be accounted as of primary importance. From his infancy, the child must be nursed at the breast of God's love, and nurtured in the embrace of His knowledge, that he may radiate light, grow in spirituality, be filled with wisdom and learning, and take on the characteristics of the angelic host.

—*'Abdu'l-Bahá*

4

While the children are yet in their infancy feed them from the breast of heavenly grace, foster them in the cradle of all excellence, rear them in the embrace of bounty. Give them the advantage of every useful kind of knowledge. Let them share in every new and rare and wondrous craft and art. Bring them up to work and strive, and accustom them to hardship. Teach them to dedicate their lives to matters of great import, and inspire them to undertake studies that will benefit mankind.

— *'Abdu'l-Bahá*

5

Children must be most carefully watched over, protected and trained; in such consisteth true parenthood and parental mercy.

—*'Abdu'l-Bahá*

Motherhood

6

Let the mothers consider that whatever concerneth the education of children is of the first importance. Let them put forth every effort in this regard, for when the bough is green and tender it will grow in whatever way ye train it. Therefore is it incumbent upon the mothers to rear their little ones even as a gardener tendeth his young plants. Let them strive by day and by night to establish within their children faith and certitude, the fear of God, the love of the Beloved of the worlds, and all good qualities and traits. Whensoever a mother seeth that her child hath done well, let her praise and applaud him and cheer his heart; and if the slightest undesirable trait should manifest itself, let her counsel the child and punish him, and use means based on reason, even a slight verbal chastisement should this be necessary. It is not, however, permissible to strike a child, or vilify him, for the child's character will be totally perverted if he be subjected to blows or verbal abuse.

—'Abdu'l-Bahá

7

O handmaids of the Merciful! Render ye thanks unto the Ancient Beauty* that ye have been raised up and gathered together in this mightiest of centuries, this most illumined of ages. As befitting thanks for such a bounty, stand ye staunch and strong in the Covenant† and, following the precepts of God and the holy Law, suckle your children from their infancy with the milk of a universal education, and rear them so that from their earliest days, within their inmost heart, their very nature, a way of life will be firmly established that will conform to the divine Teachings in all things.

For mothers are the first educators, the first mentors; and truly it is the mothers who determine the

---

* A translation of *Jamál-i-Qadím,* a name of God that is also used as a title of Bahá'u'lláh.

† The binding agreement between God and humanity that God will provide guidance to humankind and that humankind will accept it.

happiness, the future greatness, the courteous ways and learning and judgment, the understanding and the faith of their little ones.

—*'Abdu'l-Bahá*

8

O handmaid of God! . . . To the mothers must be given the divine Teachings and effective counsel, and they must be encouraged and made eager to train their children, for the mother is the first educator of the child. It is she who must, at the very beginning, suckle the newborn at the breast of God's Faith and God's Law, that divine love may enter into him even with his mother's milk, and be with him till his final breath.

So long as the mother faileth to train her children, and start them on a proper way of life, the training which they receive later on will not take its full effect. It is incumbent . . . to provide the mothers with a well-planned program for the education of children, showing how, from infancy, the child must be watched over and taught. These instructions must be given to every mother to serve her as a guide, so that each will train and nurture her children in accordance with the Teachings.

Thus will these young plants in the garden of God's love grow and flourish under the warmth of the Sun of Truth, the gentle spring winds of Heaven, and their mother's guiding hand. Thus, in the Abhá Paradise,* will each become a tree, bearing his clustered fruit, and each one, in this new and wondrous season, out of the bounties of the spring, will become possessed of all beauty and grace.

—'Abdu'l-Bahá

9

O handmaids of the Lord! . . . Work ye for the guidance of the women in that land, teach the young girls and the children, so that the mothers may educate their little ones from their earliest days, thoroughly train them, rear them to have a goodly character and good morals, guide them to all the virtues of humankind, prevent the development of any behavior that would be worthy of blame, and foster them in the embrace of Bahá'í education.† Thus shall these tender infants be nurtured at the breast

---

* *The Most Glorious Paradise:* the spiritual world beyond this world.

† Bahá'í education focuses on the spiritual and moral training of children. This is accomplished by educating children in the teachings of the Bahá'í Faith, such as the concept of world citizenship, the elimination of prejudice, the equality of men and women, and the harmony between science and religion.

of the knowledge of God and His love. Thus shall they grow and flourish, and be taught righteousness and the dignity of humankind, resolution and the will to strive and to endure. Thus shall they learn perseverance in all things, the will to advance, high mindedness and high resolve, chastity and purity of life. Thus shall they be enabled to carry to a successful conclusion whatsoever they undertake.

—'Abdu'l-Bahá

10

O ye loving mothers, know ye that in God's sight, the best of all ways to worship Him is to educate the children and train them in all the perfections of humankind; and no nobler deed than this can be imagined.

—'Abdu'l-Bahá

Marriage

1

He is God!

O peerless Lord! In Thine almighty wisdom Thou hast enjoined marriage upon the peoples, that the generations of men may succeed one another in this contingent world, and that ever, so long as the world shall last, they may busy themselves at the Threshold of Thy oneness with servitude and worship, with salutation, adoration and praise. "I have not created spirits and men, but that they should worship me."* Wherefore, wed Thou in the heaven of Thy mercy these two birds of the nest of Thy love, and make them the means of attracting perpetual grace; that from the union of these two seas of love a wave of tenderness may surge and cast the pearls of pure and goodly issue on the shore of life. "He hath let loose the two seas, that they meet each other: Between them is a barrier which they overpass not. Which then of the bounties of your Lord will ye deny? From each He bringeth up greater and lesser pearls."†

---

* Qur'án 51:56.

† Qur'án 55:19–20.

O Thou kind Lord! Make Thou this marriage to bring forth coral and pearls. Thou art verily the All-Powerful, the Most Great, the Ever-Forgiving.

—'Abdu'l-Bahá

2

Glory be unto Thee, O my God! Verily, this Thy servant and this Thy maidservant have gathered under the shadow of Thy mercy and they are united through Thy favor and generosity. O Lord! Assist them in this Thy world and Thy kingdom and destine for them every good through Thy bounty and grace. O Lord! Confirm them in Thy servitude and assist them in Thy service. Suffer them to become the signs of Thy Name in Thy world and protect them through Thy bestowals which are inexhaustible in this world and the world to come. O Lord! They are supplicating the kingdom of Thy mercifulness and invoking the realm of Thy singleness. Verily, they are married in obedience to Thy command. Cause them to become the signs of harmony and unity until the end of time. Verily, Thou art the Omnipotent, the Omnipresent and the Almighty!

—'Abdu'l-Bahá

3

O my Lord, O my Lord! These two bright orbs are wedded in Thy love, conjoined in servitude to Thy Holy Threshold, united in ministering to Thy Cause. Make Thou this marriage to be as threading lights of Thine abounding grace, O my Lord, the All-Merciful, the luminous rays of Thy bestowals, O Thou the Beneficent, the Ever-Giving, that there may branch out from this great tree boughs that will grow green and flourishing through the gifts that rain down from Thy clouds of grace.

Verily, Thou art the Generous. Verily, Thou art the Almighty. Verily, Thou art the Compassionate, the All-Merciful.

—*'Abdu'l-Bahá*

ॐ ॐ ॐ

4

Enter into wedlock, O people, that ye may bring forth one who will make mention of Me amid My servants. This is My bidding unto you; hold fast to it as an assistance to yourselves.

—*Bahá'u'lláh*

5

He is the Bestower, the Bounteous!

Praise be to God, the Ancient, the Ever-Abiding, the Changeless, the Eternal! He Who hath testified in His Own Being that verily He is the One, the Single, the Untrammeled, the Exalted. We bear witness that verily there is no God but Him, acknowledging His oneness, confessing His singleness. He hath ever dwelt in unapproachable heights, in the summits of His loftiness, sanctified from the mention of aught save Himself, free from the description of aught but Him.

And when He desired to manifest grace and beneficence to men, and to set the world in order, He revealed observances and created laws; among them He established the law of marriage, made it as a fortress for well-being and salvation, and enjoined it upon us in that which was sent down out of the heaven of sanctity in His Most Holy Book. He saith, great is His glory: "Marry, O people, that from you may appear he who will remember Me amongst My servants; this is one of My commandments unto you; obey it as an assistance to yourselves."

—*Bahá'u'lláh*

6

Bahá'í marriage is the commitment of the two parties one to the other, and their mutual attachment of mind and heart. Each must, however, exercise the utmost care to become thoroughly acquainted with the character of the other, that the binding covenant between them may be a tie that will endure forever. Their purpose must be this: to become loving companions and comrades and at one with each other for time and eternity. . . . Husband and wife should be united both physically and spiritually, that they may ever improve the spiritual life of each other, and may enjoy everlasting unity throughout all the worlds of God.

—'Abdu'l-Bahá

7

Marriage, among the mass of the people, is a physical bond, and this union can only be temporary, since it is foredoomed to a physical separation at the close.

Among the people of Bahá,* however, marriage must be a union of the body and of the

---

* Bahá'ís.

spirit as well, for here both husband and wife are aglow with the same wine, both are enamored of the same matchless Face, both live and move through the same spirit, both are illumined by the same glory. This connection between them is a spiritual one, hence it is a bond that will abide forever. Likewise do they enjoy strong and lasting ties in the physical world as well, for if the marriage is based both on the spirit and the body, that union is a true one, hence it will endure. If, however, the bond is physical and nothing more, it is sure to be only temporary, and must inexorably end in separation.

When, therefore, the people of Bahá undertake to marry, the union must be a true relationship, a spiritual coming together as well as a physical one, so that throughout every phase of life, and in all the worlds of God, their union will endure; for this real oneness is a gleaming out of the love of God.

—'Abdu'l-Bahá

8

O ye two believers in God! The Lord, peerless is He, hath made woman and man to abide with each other in the closest companionship, and to be even as a single soul. They are two helpmates, two intimate friends, who should be concerned about the welfare of each other.

If they live thus, they will pass through this world with perfect contentment, bliss, and peace of heart, and become the object of divine grace and favor in the Kingdom of heaven. But if they do other than this, they will live out their lives in great bitterness, longing at every moment for death, and will be shamefaced in the heavenly realm.

Strive, then, to abide, heart and soul, with each other as two doves in the nest, for this is to be blessed in both worlds.

—*'Abdu'l-Bahá*

9

Surely, all must today be called to love, to unity and to kindness; to integrity, to friendship, to fellowship and to divine worship. I hope that thou and thy dear husband may continue to serve in all spirit and fragrance and that in this world ye may remain two radiant candles and from the eternal horizon ye may glisten like unto two shining stars.

—*'Abdu'l-Bahá*

Love

1

I pray Thee, O Thou Who causest the dawn to appear, by Thy Name through Which Thou hast subjected the winds, and sent down Thy Tablets, that Thou wilt grant that we may draw near unto what Thou didst destine for us by Thy favor and bounty, and to be far removed from whatsoever may be repugnant unto Thee. Give us, then, to drink from the hands of Thy grace every day and every moment of our lives of the waters that are life indeed, O Thou Who art the Most Merciful! Make us, then, to be of them who helped Thee when fallen into the hands of those Thine enemies who are numbered with the rebellious among Thy creatures and the wicked amidst Thy people. Write down, then, for us the recompense ordained for him that hath attained Thy presence, and gazed on Thy beauty, and supply us with every good thing ordained in Thy Book for such of Thy creatures as enjoy near access to Thee.

Brighten our hearts, O my Lord, with the splendor of Thy knowledge, and illumine our sight with the light of such eyes as are fixed upon the horizon of Thy grace and the Dayspring of Thy glory. Preserve us, then, by Thy Most Great Name, Which

Thou didst cause to overshadow such nations as lay claim to what Thou hast forbidden in Thy Book. This, verily, is what Thou didst announce unto us in Thy Scriptures and Thy Tablets.

Cause us, then, to be so steadfast in our love towards Thee that we will turn to none except Thee, and will be reckoned amongst them that are brought nigh to Thee, and acknowledge Thee as One Who is exalted above every comparison and is holy beyond all likeness, and will lift up our voices amongst Thy servants and cry aloud that He is the one God, the Incomparable, the Ever-Abiding, the Most Powerful, the All-Glorious, the All-Wise.

Strengthen Thou, O my Lord, the hearts of them that love Thee, that they may not be affrighted by the hosts of the infidels that are turned back from Thee, but may follow Thee in whatsoever hath been revealed by Thee. Aid them, moreover, to remember and to praise Thee, and to teach Thy Cause with eloquence and wisdom. Thou art He Who hath called Himself the Most Merciful. Ordain, then, O my God, for me and for whosoever hath sought Thee what beseemeth the excellence of Thy glory and the greatness of Thy majesty. No God is there but Thee, the Ever-Forgiving, the Most Compassionate.

—*Bahá'u'lláh*

2

P raise be to Thee, O Lord my God! I implore Thee, by Thy Name which none hath befittingly recognized, and whose import no soul hath fathomed; I beseech Thee, by Him Who is the Fountain-Head of Thy Revelation and the Dayspring of Thy signs, to make my heart to be a receptacle of Thy love and of remembrance of Thee. Knit it, then, to Thy most great Ocean, that from it may flow out the living waters of Thy wisdom and the crystal streams of Thy glorification and praise.

The limbs of my body testify to Thy unity, and the hair of my head declareth the power of Thy sovereignty and might. I have stood at the door of Thy grace with utter self-effacement and complete abnegation, and clung to the hem of Thy bounty, and fixed mine eyes upon the horizon of Thy gifts.

Do Thou destine for me, O my God, what becometh the greatness of Thy majesty, and assist me, by Thy strengthening grace, so to teach Thy Cause that the dead may speed out of their sepulchers, and rush forth towards Thee, trusting wholly in Thee, and fixing their gaze upon the orient of Thy Cause, and the dawning-place of Thy Revelation.

Thou, verily, art the Most Powerful, the Most High, the All-Knowing, the All-Wise.

—*Bahá'u'lláh*

3

Rain down . . . upon us, O my God, that which beseemeth Thy grace and befitteth Thy bounty. Enable us, then, O my God, to live in remembrance of Thee and to die in love of Thee, and supply us with the gift of Thy presence in Thy worlds hereafter—worlds which are inscrutable to all except Thee. Thou art our Lord and the Lord of all worlds, and the God of all that are in heaven and all that are on earth.

—*Bahá'u'lláh*

❧　❧　❧

4

O My servants! Deprive not yourselves of the unfading and resplendent Light that shineth within the Lamp of Divine glory. Let the flame of the love of God burn brightly within your radiant hearts. Feed it with the oil of Divine guidance, and protect it within the shelter of your constancy. Guard it within the globe of trust and detachment from all else but God, so that the evil whisperings of the ungodly may not extinguish its light. O My servants! My holy, My divinely ordained Revelation may be likened unto an ocean in whose depths are concealed innumerable pearls of great price, of surpassing luster. . . . O My servants! The one true God is My witness! This most great, this fathomless and surging Ocean is near, astonishingly near, unto you. Behold it is closer to you than your life-vein! Swift as the twinkling of an eye ye can, if ye but wish it, reach and partake of this imperishable favor, this God-given grace, this incorruptible gift, this most potent and unspeakably glorious bounty.

—*Bahá'u'lláh*

5

Know thou of a certainty that Love is the secret of God's holy Dispensation,* the manifestation of the All-Merciful, the foun-

---

* A dispensation is the period of time during which the laws and teachings of a Prophet of God have spiritual authority. The dispensation of Bahá'u'lláh began in 1852, when He experienced the first intimation of His mission, and will last until the advent of the next Manifestation of God, which Bahá'u'lláh asserts will occur in no less than one thousand years.

tain of spiritual outpourings. Love is heaven's kindly light, the Holy Spirit's eternal breath that vivifieth the human soul. Love is the cause of God's revelation unto man, the vital bond inherent, in accordance with the divine creation, in the realities of things. Love is the one means that ensureth true felicity both in this world and the next. Love is the light that guideth in darkness, the living link that uniteth God with man, that assureth the progress of every illumined soul. Love is the most great law that ruleth this mighty and heavenly cycle, the unique power that bindeth together the divers elements of this material world, the supreme magnetic force that directeth the movements of the spheres in the celestial realms. Love revealeth with unfailing and limitless power the mysteries latent in the universe. Love is the spirit of life unto the adorned body of mankind, the establisher of true civilization in this mortal world, and the shedder of imperishable glory upon every high-aiming race and nation.

—'Abdu'l-Bahá

6

Be ye the helpers of every victim of oppression, the patrons of the disadvantaged. Think ye at all times of rendering some service to every member of the human race. Pay ye no heed to aversion and rejection, to disdain, hostility, injustice: act ye in the opposite way. Be ye sincerely kind, not in appearance only. Let each one of God's loved ones center his attention on this: to be the Lord's mercy to man; to be the Lord's grace. Let him do some good to every person whose path he crosseth, and be of some benefit to him. Let him improve the character of each and all, and reorient the minds of men. In this way, the light of divine guidance will shine forth, and the blessings of God will cradle all mankind: for love is light, no matter in what abode it dwelleth; and hate is darkness, no matter where it may make its nest. O friends of God! That the hidden Mystery may stand revealed, and the secret essence of all things may be disclosed, strive ye to banish that darkness for ever and ever.

—*'Abdu'l-Bahá*

7

It is my hope that . . . day by day ye will love God in ever greater measure, and become more tightly bound to the Beauty that abideth forever, to Him Who is the Light of the world. For love of God and spiritual attraction do cleanse and purify the human heart and dress and adorn it with the spotless garment of holiness; and once the heart is entirely attached to the Lord, and bound over to the Blessed Perfection,* then will the grace of God be revealed.

This love is not of the body but completely of the soul. And those souls whose inner being is lit by the love of God are even as spreading rays of light, and they shine out like stars of holiness in a pure and crystalline sky. For true love, real love, is the love for God, and this is sanctified beyond the notions and imaginings of men.

Let God's beloved, each and every one, be the essence of purity, the very life of holiness, so that in every country they may become famed for their sanctity, independence of spirit, and meekness. Let them be cheered by drafts from the eternal cup of love for God, and make merry as they drink from the wine-vaults of Heaven. Let them behold the Blessed Beauty, and feel the flame and rapture of that meeting, and be struck dumb with awe and wonder. This is the station of the sincere; this is the way of the loyal; this is the brightness that shineth on the faces of those nigh unto God.

—'Abdu'l-Bahá

---

* A translation of *Jamál-i-Mubárak,* a title of Bahá'u'lláh.

Equality of the Sexes

1

Say: God sufficeth all things above all things, and nothing in the heavens or in the earth but God sufficeth. Verily, He is in Himself the Knower, the Sustainer, the Omnipotent.

—the Báb

❧ ❧ ❧

2

In this Day the Hand of divine grace hath removed all distinctions. The servants of God and His handmaidens are regarded on the same plane. Blessed is the servant who hath attained unto that which God hath decreed, and likewise the leaf moving in accordance with the breezes of His will. This favor is great and this station lofty. His bounties and bestowals are ever present and manifest. Who is able to offer befitting gratitude for His successive bestowals and continuous favors?

—Bahá'u'lláh

3

All should know, and in this regard attain the splendors of the sun of certitude, and be illumined thereby: Women and men have been and will always be equal in the sight of God. The Dawning-Place of the Light of God sheddeth its radiance upon all with the same effulgence. Verily God created women for men, and men for women. The most beloved of people before God are the most steadfast and those who have surpassed others in their love for God, exalted be His glory.

—Bahá'u'lláh

4

Among the teachings of Bahá'u'lláh is the equality of women and men. The world of humanity has two wings—one is women and the other men. Not until both wings are equally developed can the bird fly. Should one wing remain weak, flight is impossible. Not until the world of women becomes equal to the world of men in the acquisition of virtues and perfections, can success and prosperity be attained as they ought to be.

—'Abdu'l-Bahá

5

One of the potentialities hidden in the realm of humanity was the capability or capacity of womanhood. Through the effulgent rays of divine illumination the capacity of woman has become so awakened and manifest in this age that equality of man and woman is an established fact. . . .

The truth is that all mankind are the creatures and servants of one God, and in His estimate all are human. Man is a generic term applying to all humanity. The biblical statement "Let us make man in our image, after our likeness" does not mean that woman was not created. The image and likeness of God apply to her as well. . . .

To accept and observe a distinction which God has not intended in creation is ignorance and superstition. The fact which is to be considered, however, is that woman, having formerly been deprived, must now be allowed equal opportunities with man for education and training. There must be no difference in their education. Until the reality of equality between man and woman is fully established and attained, the highest social development of mankind is not possible.

—'Abdu'l-Bahá

6

The world of humanity consists of two parts or members: one is woman; the other is man. Until these two members are equal in strength, the oneness of humanity cannot be established, and the happiness and felicity of mankind will not be a reality. God willing, this is to be so.

—'Abdu'l-Bahá

7

In past ages it was held that woman and man were not equal—that is to say, woman was considered inferior to man, even from the standpoint of her anatomy and creation. She was considered especially inferior in intelligence, and the idea prevailed universally that it was not allowable for her to step into the arena of important affairs. In some countries man went so far as to believe and teach that woman belonged to a sphere lower than human. But in this century, which is the century of light and the revelation of mysteries, God is proving to the satisfaction of humanity that all this is ignorance and error; nay, rather, it is well established that mankind and womankind as parts of composite humanity are coequal and that no difference in estimate is allowable, for all are human. The conditions in past centuries were due to woman's lack of opportunity. She was denied the right and privilege of education and left in her undeveloped state. Naturally, she could not and did not advance. In reality, God has created all mankind, and in the estimation of God there is no distinction as to male and female. The one whose heart is pure is acceptable in His sight, be that one man or woman. God does not inquire, "Art thou woman or art thou man?" He judges human actions. If these are acceptable in the threshold of the Glorious One, man and woman will be equally recognized and rewarded.

—*'Abdu'l-Bahá*

8

Woman's lack of progress and proficiency has been due to her need of equal education and opportunity. Had she been allowed this equality, there is no doubt she would be the counterpart of man in ability and capacity. The happiness of mankind will be realized when women and men coordinate and advance equally, for each is the complement and helpmeet of the other.

—*'Abdu'l-Bahá*

9

Women have equal rights with men upon earth; in religion and society they are a very important element. As long as women are prevented from attaining their highest possibilities, so long will men be unable to achieve the greatness which might be theirs.

—'Abdu'l-Bahá

10

The world of humanity has two wings, as it were: One is the female; the other is the male. If one wing be defective, the strong perfect wing will not be capable of flight. The world of humanity has two hands. If one be imperfect, the capable hand is restricted and unable to perform its duties. God is the Creator of mankind. He has endowed both sexes with perfections and intelligence, given them physical members and organs of sense, without differentiation or distinction as to superiority; therefore, why should woman be considered inferior? This is not according to the plan and justice of God. He has created them equal; in His estimate there is no question of sex. The one whose heart is purest, whose deeds are most perfect, is acceptable to God, male or female.

—'Abdu'l-Bahá

11

In this Revelation of Bahá'u'lláh, the women go neck and neck with the men. In no movement will they be left behind. Their rights with men are equal in degree. They will enter all the administrative branches of politics. They will attain in all such a degree as will be considered the very highest station of the world of humanity and will take part in all affairs. Rest ye assured. Do ye not look upon the present conditions; in the not far distant future the world of women will become all-refulgent and all-glorious, *For His Holiness Bahá'u'lláh Hath Willed It so!* At the time of elections the right to vote is the inalienable right of women, and the entrance of women into all human departments is an irrefutable and incontrovertible question. No soul can retard or prevent it.

—*'Abdu'l-Bahá*

Unity

1

O my God! O my God! Unite the hearts of Thy servants, and reveal to them Thy great purpose. May they follow Thy commandments and abide in Thy law. Help them, O God, in their endeavor, and grant them strength to serve Thee. O God! Leave them not to themselves, but guide their steps by the light of Thy knowledge, and cheer their hearts by Thy love. Verily, Thou art their Helper and their Lord.

—Bahá'u'lláh

2

O my God! O my God! Verily, I invoke Thee and supplicate before Thy threshold, asking Thee that all Thy mercies may descend upon these souls. Specialize them for Thy favor and Thy truth.

O Lord! Unite and bind together the hearts, join in accord all the souls, and exhilarate the spirits through the signs of Thy sanctity and oneness. O Lord! Make these faces radiant through the light of Thy oneness. Strengthen the loins of Thy servants in the service of Thy kingdom.

O Lord, Thou possessor of infinite mercy! O Lord of forgiveness and pardon! Forgive our sins, pardon our shortcomings, and cause us to turn to the kingdom of Thy clemency, invoking the kingdom of might and power, humble at Thy shrine and submissive before the glory of Thine evidences.

O Lord God! Make us as waves of the sea, as flowers of the garden, united, agreed through the bounties of Thy love. O Lord! Dilate the breasts through the signs of Thy oneness, and make all mankind as stars shining from the same height of glory, as perfect fruits growing upon Thy tree of life.

Verily, Thou art the Almighty, the Self-Subsistent, the Giver, the Forgiving, the Pardoner, the Omniscient, the One Creator.

—'Abdu'l-Bahá

❧ ❧ ❧

3

O ye children of men! The fundamental purpose animating the Faith of God and His Religion is to safeguard the interests and promote the unity of the human race, and to foster the spirit of love and fellowship amongst men. . . . This is the straight Path, the fixed and immovable foundation. Whatsoever is raised on this foundation, the changes and chances of the world can never impair its strength, nor will the revolution of countless centuries undermine its structure.

—*Bahá'u'lláh*

4

The Great Being saith: O well-beloved ones! The tabernacle of unity hath been raised; regard ye not one another as strangers. Ye are the fruits of one tree, and the leaves of one branch.

—*Bahá'u'lláh*

5

O ye beloved of the Lord! Commit not that which defileth the limpid stream of love or destroyeth the sweet fragrance of friendship. By the righteousness of the Lord! Ye were created to show love one to another and not perversity and rancor. Take pride not in love for yourselves but in love for your fellow creatures. Glory not in love for your country, but in love for all mankind.

—*Bahá'u'lláh*

6

Today the most remarkable favor of God centereth around union and harmony among the friends; so that this unity and concord may be the cause of the promulgation of the oneness of the world of humanity, may emancipate the world from this intense darkness of enmity and rancor, and that the Sun of Truth may shine in full and perfect effulgence.

Today, all the peoples of the world are indulging in self-interest and exert the utmost effort and endeavor to promote their own material interests. They are worshiping themselves and not the divine reality, nor the world of mankind. They seek diligently their own benefit and not the commonweal. This is because they are captives of the world of nature and unaware of the divine teachings, of the bounty of the Kingdom and of the Sun of Truth.

—*'Abdu'l-Bahá*

7

In the world of existence there are various bonds which unite human hearts, but not one of these bonds is completely effective. The first and foremost is the bond of family relationship, which is not an efficient unity, for how often it happens that disagreement and divergence rend asunder this close tie of association. The bond of patriotism may be a means of fellowship and agreement, but oneness of native land will not completely cement human hearts; for if we review history, we shall find that people of the same race and native land have frequently waged war against each other. Often in civil strife they have shed the same racial blood and destroyed the possessions of their own native kind. Therefore, this bond is not sufficient. Another means of seeming unity is the bond of political association, where governments and rulers have been allied for reasons of intercourse and mutual protection, but which agreement and union afterward became subject to change and violent hatred even to the extreme of war and bloodshed. It is evident that political oneness is not permanently effective.

The source of perfect unity and love in the world of existence is the bond and oneness of reality. When the divine and fundamental reality enters human hearts and lives, it conserves and protects all states and conditions of mankind, establishing that intrinsic oneness of the world of humanity which can only come into being through the efficacy of the Holy Spirit. For the Holy Spirit is like unto the life in the human body, which blends all differences of parts and members in unity and agreement. Consider how numerous are these parts and members, but the oneness of the animating spirit of life unites them all in perfect combination. It establishes such a unity in the bodily organism that if any part is subjected to injury or becomes diseased, all the other parts and functions sympathetically respond and suffer, owing to the perfect oneness existing. Just as the human spirit of life is the cause of coordination among the various parts of the human organism, the Holy Spirit is the controlling cause of the unity and coordination of mankind. That is to say, the bond or oneness of humanity cannot be effectively established save through the power of the Holy Spirit, for the world of humanity is a composite body, and the Holy Spirit is the animating principle of its life.

—'Abdu'l-Bahá

8

Be in perfect unity. Never become angry with one another. Let your eyes be directed toward the kingdom of truth and not toward the world of creation. Love the creatures for the sake of God and not for themselves. You will never become angry or impatient if you love them for the sake of God. Humanity is not perfect. There are imperfections in every human being, and you will always become unhappy if you look toward the people themselves. But if you look toward God, you will love them and be kind to them, for the world of God is the world of perfection and complete mercy. Therefore, do not look at the shortcomings of anybody; see with the sight of forgiveness. The imperfect eye beholds imperfections. The eye that covers faults looks toward the Creator of souls. He created them, trains and provides for them, endows them with capacity and life, sight and hearing; therefore, they are the signs of His grandeur. You must love and be kind to everybody, care for the poor, protect the weak, heal the sick, teach and educate the ignorant.

—*'Abdu'l-Bahá*

9

The Blessed Beauty* saith: "Ye are all the fruits of one tree, the leaves of one branch." Thus hath He likened this world of being to a single tree, and all its peoples to the leaves thereof, and the blossoms and fruits. It is needful for the bough to blossom, and the leaf and fruit to flourish, and upon the interconnection of all parts of the world-tree, dependeth the flourishing of leaf and blossom, and the sweetness of the fruit.

For this reason must all human beings powerfully sustain one another and seek for everlasting

---

* A translation of *Jamál-i-Mubárak,* a title of Bahá'u'lláh.

life; and for this reason must the lovers of God in this contingent world become the mercies and the blessings sent forth by that clement King of the seen and unseen realms. Let them purify their sight and behold all humankind as leaves and blossoms and fruits of the tree of being. Let them at all times concern themselves with doing a kindly thing for one of their fellows, offering to someone love, consideration, thoughtful help. Let them see no one as their enemy, or as wishing them ill, but think of all humankind as their friends; regarding the alien as an intimate, the stranger as a companion, staying free of prejudice, drawing no lines.

In this day, the one favored at the Threshold of the Lord is he who handeth round the cup of faithfulness; who bestoweth, even upon his enemies, the jewel of bounty, and lendeth, even to his fallen oppressor, a helping hand; it is he who will, even to the fiercest of his foes, be a loving friend. These are the Teachings of the Blessed Beauty, these the counsels of the Most Great Name.*

—'Abdu'l-Bahá

---

* Bahá'u'lláh.

10

Consider the flowers of a garden: though differing in kind, color, form and shape, yet, inasmuch as they are refreshed by the waters of one spring, revived by the breath of one wind, invigorated by the rays of one sun, this diversity increaseth their charm, and addeth unto their beauty. Thus when that unifying force, the penetrating influence of the Word of God, taketh effect, the difference of customs, manners, habits, ideas, opinions and dispositions embellish the world of humanity. This diversity, this difference is like the naturally created dissimilarity and variety of the limbs and organs of the human body, for each one contributeth to the beauty, efficiency and perfection of the whole. When these different limbs and organs come under the influence of man's sovereign soul, and the soul's power pervadeth the limbs and members, veins and arteries of the body, then difference reinforceth harmony, diversity strengtheneth love, and multiplicity is the greatest factor for coordination.

How unpleasing to the eye if all the flowers and plants, the leaves and blossoms, the fruits, the branches and the trees of that garden were all of the same shape and color! Diversity of hues, form and shape, enricheth and adorneth the garden, and heighteneth the effect thereof. In like manner, when divers shades of thought, temperament and character, are brought together under the power and influence of one central agency, the beauty and glory of human perfection will be revealed and made manifest. Naught but the celestial potency of the Word of God, which ruleth and transcendeth the realities of all things, is capable of harmonizing the divergent thoughts, sentiments, ideas, and convictions of the children of men. Verily, it is the penetrating power in all things, the mover of souls and the binder and regulator in the world of humanity.

—'Abdu'l-Bahá

11

Reflect ye as to other than human forms of life and be ye admonished thereby: those clouds that drift apart cannot produce the bounty of the rain, and are soon lost; a flock of sheep, once scattered, falleth prey to the wolf, and birds that fly alone will be caught fast in the claws of the hawk. What greater demonstration could there be that unity leadeth to flourishing life, while dissension and withdrawing from the others, will lead only to misery; for these are the sure ways to bitter disappointment and ruin.

—'Abdu'l-Bahá

Praise and Thanksgiving

1

My God, my Adored One, my King, my Desire! What tongue can voice my thanks to Thee? I was heedless, Thou didst awaken me. I had turned back from Thee, Thou didst graciously aid me to turn towards Thee. I was as one dead, Thou didst quicken me with the water of life. I was withered, Thou didst revive me with the heavenly stream of Thine utterance which hath flowed forth from the Pen of the All-Merciful.

O Divine Providence! All existence is begotten by Thy bounty; deprive it not of the waters of Thy generosity, neither do Thou withhold it from the ocean of Thy mercy. I beseech Thee to aid and assist me at all times and under all conditions, and seek from the heaven of Thy grace Thine ancient favor. Thou art, in truth, the Lord of bounty, and the Sovereign of the kingdom of eternity.

—*Bahá'u'lláh*

2

I bear witness, O my God, that Thou hast created me to know Thee and to worship Thee.

I testify, at this moment, to my powerlessness and to Thy might, to my poverty and to Thy wealth.

There is none other God but Thee, the Help in Peril, the Self-Subsisting.

—*Bahá'u'lláh*

3

I know not, O my God, what the Fire is which Thou didst kindle in Thy land. Earth can never cloud its splendor, nor water quench its flame. All the peoples of the world are powerless to resist its force. Great is the blessedness of him that hath drawn nigh unto it, and heard its roaring.

Some, O my God, Thou didst, through Thy strengthening grace, enable to approach it, while others Thou didst keep back by reason of what their hands have wrought in Thy days. Whoso hath hasted towards it and attained unto it hath, in his eagerness to gaze on Thy beauty, yielded his life in Thy path, and ascended unto Thee, wholly detached from aught else except Thyself.

I beseech Thee, O my Lord, by this fire which blazeth and rageth in the world of creation, to rend asunder the veils that have hindered me from appearing before the throne of Thy majesty, and from standing at the door of Thy gate. Do Thou ordain for me, O my Lord, every good thing Thou didst send down in Thy Book, and suffer me not to be far removed from the shelter of Thy mercy.

Powerful art Thou to do what pleaseth Thee. Thou art, verily, the All-Powerful, the Most Generous.

—*Bahá'u'lláh*

4

Praise be unto Thee, O my God! I am one of Thy servants, who hath believed on Thee and on Thy signs. Thou seest how I have set myself towards the door of Thy mercy, and turned my face in the direction of Thy loving-kindness. I beseech Thee, by Thy most excellent titles and Thy most exalted attributes, to open to my face the portals of Thy bestowals. Aid me, then, to do that which is good, O Thou Who art the Possessor of all names and attributes!

I am poor, O my Lord, and Thou art the Rich. I have set my face towards Thee, and detached myself from all but Thee. Deprive me not, I implore Thee, of the breezes of Thy tender mercy, and withhold not from me what Thou didst ordain for the chosen among Thy servants.

Remove the veil from mine eyes, O my Lord, that I may recognize what Thou hast desired for Thy creatures, and discover, in all the manifestations of Thy handiwork, the revelations of Thine almighty power. Enrapture my soul, O my Lord, with Thy most mighty signs, and draw me out of the depths of my corrupt and evil desires. Write down, then, for me the good of this world and of the world to come. Potent art Thou to do what pleaseth Thee. No God is there but Thee, the All-Glorious, Whose help is sought by all men.

I yield Thee thanks, O my Lord, that Thou hast wakened me from my sleep, and stirred me up, and created in me the desire to perceive what most of Thy servants have failed to apprehend. Make me able, therefore, O my Lord, to behold, for love of Thee and for the sake of Thy pleasure, whatsoever Thou hast desired. Thou art He to the power of Whose might and sovereignty all things testify.

There is none other God but Thee, the Almighty, the Beneficent.

—*Bahá'u'lláh*

5

How can I choose to sleep, O God, my God, when the eyes of them that long for Thee are wakeful because of their separation from Thee; and how can I lie down to rest whilst the souls of Thy lovers are sore vexed in their remoteness from Thy presence?

I have committed, O my Lord, my spirit and my entire being into the right hand of Thy might and Thy protection, and I lay my head on my pillow through Thy power, and lift it up according to Thy will and Thy good pleasure. Thou art, in truth, the Preserver, the Keeper, the Almighty, the Most Powerful.

By Thy might! I ask not, whether sleeping or waking, but that which Thou dost desire. I am Thy servant and in Thy hands. Do Thou graciously aid me to do what will shed forth the fragrance of Thy good pleasure. This, truly, is my hope and the hope of them that enjoy near access to Thee. Praised be Thou, O Lord of the worlds!

—*Bahá'u'lláh*

6

All praise, O my God, be to Thee Who art the Source of all glory and majesty, of greatness and honor, of sovereignty and dominion, of loftiness and grace, of awe and power. Whomsoever Thou willest Thou causest to draw nigh unto the Most Great Ocean, and on whomsoever Thou desirest Thou conferrest the honor of recognizing Thy Most Ancient Name. Of all who are in heaven and on earth, none can withstand the operation of Thy sovereign Will. From all eternity Thou didst rule the entire creation, and Thou wilt continue for evermore to exercise Thy dominion over all created things. There is none other God but Thee, the Almighty, the Most Exalted, the All-Powerful, the All-Wise.

Illumine, O Lord, the faces of Thy servants, that they may behold Thee; and cleanse their hearts that they may turn unto the court of Thy heavenly favors, and recognize Him Who is the Manifestation of Thy Self and the Dayspring of Thine Essence. Verily, Thou art the Lord of all worlds. There is no God but Thee, the Unconstrained, the All-Subduing.

—Bahá'u'lláh

7

In the Name of God, the Most High! Lauded and glorified art Thou, Lord, God Omnipotent! Thou before Whose wisdom the wise falleth short and faileth, before Whose knowledge the learned confesseth his ignorance, before Whose might the strong waxeth weak, before Whose wealth the rich testifieth to his poverty, before Whose light the enlightened is lost in darkness, toward the shrine of Whose knowledge turneth the essence of all understanding and around the sanctuary of Whose presence circle the souls of all mankind.

How then can I sing and tell of Thine Essence, which the wisdom of the wise and the learning of the learned have failed to comprehend, inasmuch as no man can sing that which he understandeth not, nor recount that unto which he cannot attain, whilst Thou hast been from everlasting the Inaccessible, the Unsearchable. Powerless though I be to rise to the heavens of Thy glory and soar in the realms of Thy knowledge, I can but recount Thy tokens that tell of Thy glorious handiwork.

By Thy Glory! O Beloved of all hearts, Thou that alone canst still the pangs of yearning for Thee! Though all the dwellers of heaven and earth unite to glorify the least of Thy signs, wherein and whereby Thou hast revealed Thyself, yet would they fail, how much more to praise Thy holy Word, the creator of all Thy tokens.

All praise and glory be to Thee, Thou of Whom all things have testified that Thou art one and there is none other God but Thee, Who hast been from everlasting exalted above all peer or likeness and to everlasting shalt remain the same. All kings are but Thy servants and all beings, visible and invisible, as naught before Thee. There is none other God but Thee, the Gracious, the Powerful, the Most High.

—Bahá'u'lláh

8

Magnified be Thy name, O Lord my God! Thou art He Whom all things worship and Who worshipeth no one, Who is the Lord of all things and is the vassal of none, Who knoweth all things and is known of none. Thou didst wish to make Thyself known unto men; therefore, Thou didst, through a word of Thy mouth, bring creation into being and fashion the universe. There is none other God except Thee, the Fashioner, the Creator, the Almighty, the Most Powerful.

I implore Thee, by this very word that hath shone forth above the horizon of Thy will, to enable me to drink deep of the living waters through which Thou hast vivified the hearts of Thy chosen ones and quickened the souls of them that love Thee, that I may, at all times and under all conditions, turn my face wholly towards Thee.

Thou art the God of power, of glory and bounty. No God is there beside Thee, the Supreme Ruler, the All-Glorious, the Omniscient.

—*Bahá'u'lláh*

9

Glory to Thee, O my God! The first stirrings of the spring of Thy grace have appeared and clothed Thine earth with verdure. The clouds of the heaven of Thy bounty have rained their rain on this City within whose walls is imprisoned Him Whose desire is the salvation of Thy creatures. Through it the soil of this City hath been decked forth, and its trees clothed with foliage, and its inhabitants gladdened.

The hearts of Thy dear ones, however, will rejoice only at the Divine Springtime of Thy tender mercies, whereby the hearts are quickened, and the souls are renewed, and the trees of human existence bear their fruits.

The plants that have sprung forth, O my Lord, in the hearts of Thy loved ones have withered away. Send down upon them, from the clouds of Thy spirit, that which will cause the tender herbs of Thy knowledge and wisdom to grow within their breasts. Rejoice, then, their hearts with the proclamation of Thy Cause and the exaltation of Thy sovereignty.

Their eyes, O my Lord, are expectantly turned in the direction of Thy bounty, and their faces are set towards the horizon of Thy grace. Suffer them not, through Thy bounty, to be deprived of Thy grace. Potent art Thou, by Thy sovereign might, over all things. No God is there but Thee, the Almighty, the Help in Peril, the Self-Subsisting.

—*Bahá'u'lláh*

10

Praised be Thou, O Lord my God! Every time I attempt to make mention of Thee, I am hindered by the sublimity of Thy station and the overpowering greatness of Thy might. For were I to praise Thee throughout the length of Thy dominion and the duration of Thy sovereignty, I would find that my praise of Thee can befit only such as are like unto me, who are themselves Thy creatures, and who have been generated through the power of Thy decree and been fashioned through the potency of Thy will. And at whatever time my pen ascribeth glory to any one of Thy names, methinks I can hear the voice of its lamentation in its remoteness from Thee, and can recognize its cry because of its separation from Thy Self. I testify that everything other than Thee is but Thy creation and is held in the hollow of Thy hand. To have accepted any act or praise from Thy creatures is but an evidence of the wonders of Thy grace and bountiful favors, and a manifestation of Thy generosity and providence.

I entreat Thee, O my Lord, by Thy Most Great Name whereby Thou didst separate light from fire, and truth from denial, to send down upon me and upon such of my loved ones as are in my company the good of this world and of the next. Supply us, then, with Thy wondrous gifts that are hid from the eyes of men. Thou art, verily, the Fashioner of all creation. No God is there but Thee, the Almighty, the All-Glorious, the Most High.

—*Bahá'u'lláh*

11

Glory be unto Thee, O God. How can I make mention of Thee while Thou art sanctified from the praise of all mankind. Magnified be Thy Name, O God, Thou art the King, the Eternal Truth; Thou knowest what is in the heavens and on the earth, and unto Thee must all return. Thou hast sent down Thy divinely ordained Revelation according to a clear measure. Praised art Thou, O Lord! At Thy behest Thou dost render victorious whomsoever Thou willest, through the hosts of heaven and earth and whatsoever existeth between them. Thou art the Sovereign, the Eternal Truth, the Lord of invincible might.

Glorified art Thou, O Lord, Thou forgivest at all times the sins of such among Thy servants as implore Thy pardon. Wash away my sins and the sins of those who seek Thy forgiveness at dawn, who pray to Thee in the daytime and in the night season, who yearn after naught save God, who offer up whatsoever God hath graciously bestowed upon them, who celebrate Thy praise at morn and eventide, and who are not remiss in their duties.

—The Báb

12

O my God! O my God! Verily, these servants are turning to Thee, supplicating Thy kingdom of mercy. Verily, they are attracted by Thy holiness and set aglow with the fire of Thy love, seeking confirmation from Thy wondrous kingdom, and hoping for attainment in Thy heavenly realm. Verily, they long for the descent of Thy bestowal, desiring illumination from the Sun of Reality. O Lord! Make them radiant lamps, merciful signs, fruitful trees and shining stars. May they come forth in Thy service and be connected with Thee by the bonds and ties of Thy love, longing for the lights of Thy favor. O Lord! Make them signs of guidance, standards of Thine immortal kingdom, waves of the sea of Thy mercy, mirrors of the light of Thy majesty.

Verily, Thou art the Generous. Verily, Thou art the Merciful. Verily, Thou art the Precious, the Beloved.

—'Abdu'l-Bahá

13

O my Lord! I have drawn nigh unto Thee, in the depths of this darksome night, confiding in Thee with the tongue of my heart, trembling with joy at the sweet scents that blow from Thy realm, the All-Glorious, calling unto Thee, saying:

O my Lord, no words do I find to glorify Thee; no way do I see for the bird of my mind to soar upward to Thy Kingdom of Holiness; for Thou, in Thy very essence, art sanctified above those tributes, and in Thy very being art beyond the reach of those praises which are offered Thee by the people that Thou hast created. In the sanctity of Thine own being hast Thou ever been exalted above the understanding of the learned among the Company on high, and forever wilt Thou remain enwrapped within the holiness of Thine own reality, unreached by the knowledge of those dwellers in Thine exalted Kingdom who glorify Thy Name.

O God, my God! How can I glorify or describe Thee inaccessible as Thou art; immeasurably high and sanctified art Thou above every description and praise.

O God, my God! Have mercy then upon my helpless state, my poverty, my misery, my abasement! Give me to drink from the generous cup of Thy grace and forgiveness, stir me with the sweet scents of Thy love, gladden my bosom with the light of Thy knowledge, purify my soul with the mysteries of Thy oneness, raise me to life with the gentle breeze that cometh from the gardens of Thy mercy—till I sever myself from all else but Thee, and lay hold of the hem of Thy garment of grandeur, and consign to oblivion all that is not Thee, and be companioned by the sweet breathings that waft during these Thy days, and attain unto faithfulness at Thy Threshold of Holiness, and arise to serve Thy Cause, and to be humble before Thy loved ones, and, in the presence of Thy favored ones, to be nothingness itself.

Verily art Thou the Helper, the Sustainer, the Exalted, the Most Generous.

—'Abdu'l-Bahá

14

Praise be to Him through Whose splendors the earth and the heavens are aglow, through Whose fragrant breathings the gardens of holiness that adorn the hearts of the chosen are trembling for joy, to Him Who hath shed His light and brightened the face of the firmament. Verily there appeared luminous and sparkling stars, glittering, shining out, and casting forth their rays upon the supreme horizon. They derived their grace and brilliance from the bounties of the Abhá Realm, then, stars of guidance, they poured down their lights upon this earth.

Praise be to Him Who hath fashioned this new era, this age of majesty, even as an unfolding pageant where the realities of all things can be exposed to view. Now are clouds of bounty raining down and the gifts of the loving Lord are clearly manifest; for both the seen and the unseen worlds have been illumined, and the Promised One hath come to earth and the beauty of the Adored One hath shone forth.

—'Abdu'l-Bahá

15

O Thou kind Lord! Praise be unto Thee that Thou hast shown us the highway of guidance, opened the doors of the kingdom and manifested Thyself through the Sun of Reality. To the blind Thou hast given sight; to the deaf Thou hast granted hearing; Thou hast resuscitated the dead; Thou hast enriched the poor; Thou hast shown the way to those who have gone astray; Thou hast led those with parched lips to the fountain of guidance; Thou hast suffered the thirsty fish to reach the ocean of reality; and Thou hast invited the wandering birds to the rose garden of grace.

O Thou Almighty! We are Thy servants and Thy poor ones; we are remote and yearn for Thy presence, are athirst for the water of Thy fountain, are ill, longing for Thy healing. We are walking in Thy path and have no aim or hope save the diffusion of Thy fragrance, so that all souls may raise the cry of "O God, guide us to the straight path." May their eyes be opened to behold the light, and may they be freed from the darkness of ignorance. May they gather around the lamp of Thy guidance. May every portionless one receive a share. May the deprived become the confidants of Thy mysteries.

O Almighty! Look upon us with the glance of mercifulness. Grant us heavenly confirmation. Bestow upon us the breath of the Holy Spirit, so that we may be assisted in Thy service and, like unto brilliant stars, shine in these regions with the light of Thy guidance.

Verily, Thou art the Powerful, the Mighty, the Wise and the Seeing.

—'Abdu'l-Bahá

৯৯ ৯৯ ৯৯

16

We must give praise unto God, for it is the light of His bounty which has shone upon us through His love which is everlasting. His divine Manifestations have offered Their lives through love for us.

—'Abdu'l-Bahá

17

There is one God; mankind is one; the foundations of religion are one. Let us worship Him, and give praise for all His great Prophets and Messengers who have manifested His brightness and glory.

The blessing of the Eternal One be with you in all its richness, that each soul according to his measure may take freely of Him.

—'Abdu'l-Bahá

18

I beseech God to graciously make of thy home a center for the diffusion of the light of divine guidance, for the dissemination of the Words of God and for enkindling at all times the fire of love in the hearts of His faithful servants and maidservants. Know thou of a certainty that every house wherein the anthem of praise is raised to the Realm of Glory in celebration of the Name of God is indeed a heavenly home, and one of the gardens of delight in the Paradise of God.

—'Abdu'l-Bahá

Guidance

1

He is the Mighty, the Pardoner, the Compassionate!

O God, my God! Thou beholdest Thy servants in the abyss of perdition and error; where is Thy light of divine guidance, O Thou the Desire of the world? Thou knowest their helplessness and their feebleness; where is Thy power, O Thou in Whose grasp lie the powers of heaven and earth?

I ask Thee, O Lord my God, by the splendor of the lights of Thy loving-kindness and the billows of the ocean of Thy knowledge and wisdom and by Thy Word wherewith Thou hast swayed the peoples of Thy dominion, to grant that I may be one of them that have observed Thy bidding in Thy Book. And do Thou ordain for me that which Thou hast ordained for Thy trusted ones, them that have quaffed the wine of divine inspiration from the chalice of Thy bounty and hastened to do Thy pleasure and observe Thy Covenant and Testament. Powerful art Thou to do as Thou willest. There is none other God but Thee, the All-Knowing, the All-Wise.

Decree for me, by Thy bounty, O Lord, that which shall prosper me in this world and hereafter and shall draw me nigh unto Thee, O Thou Who art the Lord of all men. There is none other God but Thee, the One, the Mighty, the Glorified.

—*Bahá'u'lláh*

2

Say: Magnified be Thy Name, O Lord my God! I beseech Thee by Thy Name through which the splendor of the light of wisdom shone resplendent when the heavens of divine utterance were set in motion amidst mankind, to graciously aid me by Thy heavenly confirmations and enable me to extol Thy Name amongst Thy servants.

O Lord! Unto Thee have I turned my face, detached from all save Thee and holding fast to the hem of the robe of Thy manifold blessings. Unloose my tongue therefore to proclaim that which will captivate the minds of men and will rejoice their souls and spirits. Strengthen me then in Thy Cause in such wise that I may not be hindered by the ascendancy of the oppressors among Thy creatures nor withheld by the onslaught of the disbelievers amidst those who dwell in Thy realm. Make me as a lamp shining throughout Thy lands that those in whose hearts the light of Thy knowledge gloweth and the yearning for Thy love lingereth may be guided by its radiance.

Verily, potent art Thou to do whatsoever Thou willest, and in Thy grasp Thou holdest the kingdom of creation. There is none other God but Thee, the Almighty, the All-Wise.

—*Bahá'u'lláh*

3

Glory be to Thee, O Lord my God! Make manifest the rivers of Thy sovereign might, that the waters of Thy Unity may flow through the inmost realities of all things, in such wise that the banner of Thine unfailing guidance may be raised aloft in the kingdom of Thy command and the stars of Thy divine splendor may shine brightly in the heaven of Thy majesty.

Potent art Thou to do what pleaseth Thee. Thou, verily, art the Help in Peril, the Self-Subsisting.

—*Bahá'u'lláh*

4

O Lord my God! Assist Thy loved ones to be firm in Thy Faith, to walk in Thy ways, to be steadfast in Thy Cause. Give them Thy grace to withstand the onslaught of self and passion, to follow the light of divine guidance. Thou art the Powerful, the Gracious, the Self-Subsisting, the Bestower, the Compassionate, the Almighty, the All-Bountiful.

—*'Abdu'l-Bahá*

5

O God, O Thou Who hast cast Thy splendor over the luminous realities of men, shedding upon them the resplendent lights of knowledge and guidance, and hast chosen them out of all created things for this supernal grace, and hast caused them to encompass all things, to understand their inmost essence, and to disclose their mysteries, bringing them forth out of darkness into the visible world! "He verily showeth His special mercy to whomsoever He will."*

O Lord, help Thou Thy loved ones to acquire knowledge and the sciences and arts, and to unravel the secrets that are treasured up in the inmost reality of all created beings. Make them to hear the hidden truths that are written and embedded in the heart of all that is. Make them to be ensigns of guidance amongst all creatures, and piercing rays of the mind shedding forth their light in this, the "first life."† Make them to be leaders unto Thee, guides unto Thy path, runners urging men on to Thy Kingdom.

Thou verily art the Powerful, the Protector, the Potent, the Defender, the Mighty, the Most Generous.

—'Abdu'l-Bahá

---

* Qur'án 3:67.
† Qur'án 56:62.

6

O compassionate God! Thanks be to Thee for Thou hast awakened and made me conscious. Thou hast given me a seeing eye and favored me with a hearing ear, hast led me to Thy kingdom and guided me to Thy path. Thou hast shown me the right way and caused me to enter the ark of deliverance. O God! Keep me steadfast and make me firm and staunch. Protect me from violent tests and preserve and shelter me in the strongly fortified fortress of Thy Covenant and Testament. Thou art the Powerful. Thou art the Seeing. Thou art the Hearing.

O Thou the Compassionate God. Bestow upon me a heart which, like unto a glass, may be illumined with the light of Thy love, and confer upon me thoughts which may change this world into a rose garden through the outpourings of heavenly grace.

Thou art the Compassionate, the Merciful. Thou art the Great Beneficent God.

—'Abdu'l-Bahá

7

O my Lord and my Hope! Help Thou Thy loved ones to be steadfast in Thy mighty Covenant, to remain faithful to Thy manifest Cause, and to carry out the commandments

Thou didst set down for them in Thy Book of Splendors; that they may become banners of guidance and lamps of the Company above, wellsprings of Thine infinite wisdom, and stars that lead aright, as they shine down from the supernal sky.

Verily, art Thou the Invincible, the Almighty, the All-Powerful.

—'Abdu'l-Bahá

8

O Thou, my God, Who guidest the seeker to the pathway that leadeth aright, Who deliverest the lost and blinded soul out of the wastes of perdition, Thou Who bestowest upon the sincere great bounties and favors, Who guardest the frightened within Thine impregnable refuge, Who answerest, from Thine all-highest horizon, the cry of those who cry out unto Thee. Praised be Thou, O my Lord! Thou hast guided the distracted out of the death of unbelief, and hast brought those who draw nigh unto Thee to the journey's goal, and hast rejoiced the assured among Thy servants by granting them their most cherished desires, and hast, from Thy Kingdom of beauty, opened before the faces of those who yearn after Thee the gates of reunion, and hast rescued them from the fires of deprivation and loss—so that they hastened unto Thee and gained Thy presence, and arrived at Thy welcoming door, and received of gifts an abundant share.

O my Lord, they thirsted, Thou didst lift to their parched lips the waters of reunion. O Tender One, Bestowing One, Thou didst calm their pain with the balm of Thy bounty and grace, and didst heal their ailments with the sovereign medicine of Thy compassion. O Lord, make firm their feet on Thy straight path, make wide for them the needle's eye, and cause them, dressed in royal robes, to walk in glory for ever and ever.

Verily, art Thou the Generous, the Ever-Giving, the Precious, the Most Bountiful. There is none other God but Thee, the Mighty, the Powerful, the Exalted, the Victorious.

—*'Abdu'l-Bahá*

9

O God, guide me, protect me, make of me a shining lamp and a brilliant star. Thou art the Mighty and the Powerful.

—*'Abdu'l-Bahá*

ক ক ক

10

The Prophets and Messengers of God have been sent down for the sole purpose of guiding mankind to the straight Path of Truth. The purpose underlying Their revelation hath been to educate all men, that they may, at the hour of death, ascend, in the utmost purity and sanctity and with absolute detachment, to the throne of the Most High. The light which these souls radiate is responsible for the progress of the world and the advancement of its peoples. They are like unto leaven which leaveneth the world of being, and constitute the animating force through which the arts and wonders of the world are made manifest.

—*Bahá'u'lláh*

11

Pray to God that He may strengthen you in divine virtue, so that you may be as angels in the world, and beacons of light to disclose the mysteries of the Kingdom to those with understanding hearts.

God sent His Prophets into the world to teach and enlighten man, to explain to him the mystery of the Power of the Holy Spirit, to enable him to reflect the light, and so in his turn, to be the source of guidance to others. The Heavenly Books, the

Bible, the Qur'án, and the other Holy Writings have been given by God as guides into the paths of Divine virtue, love, justice and peace.

Therefore I say unto you that ye should strive to follow the counsels of these Blessed Books, and so order your lives that ye may, following the examples set before you, become yourselves the saints of the Most High!

—'Abdu'l-Bahá

12

As the East and the West are illumined by one sun, so all races, nations, and creeds shall be seen as the servants of the One God. The whole earth is one home, and all peoples, did they but know it, are bathed in the oneness of God's mercy. God created all. He gives sustenance to all. He guides and trains all under the shadow of his bounty. We must follow the example God Himself gives us, and do away with all disputations and quarrels.

—'Abdu'l-Bahá

13

I ask you all, each one of you, to follow well the light of truth, in the Holy Teachings, and God will strengthen you by His Holy Spirit so that you will be enabled to overcome the difficulties, and to destroy the prejudices which cause separation and hatred amongst the people. Let your hearts be filled with the great love of God, let it be felt by all; for every man is a servant of God, and all are entitled to a share of the Divine Bounty.

—*'Abdu'l-Bahá*

Spiritual Growth

1

Attire, O my Lord, both my inner and outer being with the raiment of Thy favors and Thy loving-kindness. Keep me safe, then, from whatsoever may be abhorrent unto Thee, and graciously assist me and my kindred to obey Thee, and to shun whatsoever may stir up any evil or corrupt desire within me.

Thou, truly, art the Lord of all mankind, and the Possessor of this world and of the next. No God is there save Thee, the All-Knowing, the All-Wise.

—*Bahá'u'lláh*

2

From the sweet-scented streams of Thine eternity give me to drink, O my God, and of the fruits of the tree of Thy being enable me to taste, O my Hope! From the crystal springs of Thy love suffer me to quaff, O my Glory, and beneath the shadow of Thine everlasting providence let me abide, O my Light! Within the meadows of Thy nearness, before Thy presence, make me able to roam, O my Beloved, and at the right hand of the throne of Thy mercy, seat me, O my Desire! From the fragrant breezes of

Thy joy let a breath pass over me, O my Goal, and into the heights of the paradise of Thy reality let me gain admission, O my Adored One! To the melodies of the dove of Thy oneness suffer me to hearken, O Resplendent One, and through the spirit of Thy power and Thy might quicken me, O my Provider! In the spirit of Thy love keep me steadfast, O my Succorer, and in the path of Thy good pleasure set firm my steps, O my Maker! Within the garden of Thine immortality, before Thy countenance, let me abide for ever, O Thou Who art merciful unto me, and upon the seat of Thy glory stablish me, O Thou Who art my Possessor! To the heaven of Thy loving-kindness lift me up, O my Quickener, and unto the Daystar of Thy guidance lead me, O Thou my Attractor! Before the revelations of Thine invisible spirit summon me to be present, O Thou Who art my Origin and my Highest Wish, and unto the essence of the fragrance of Thy beauty, which Thou wilt manifest, cause me to return, O Thou Who art my God!

Potent art Thou to do what pleaseth Thee. Thou art, verily, the Most Exalted, the All-Glorious, the All-Highest.

—Bahá'u'lláh

3

O my Lord! Make Thy beauty to be my food, and Thy presence my drink, and Thy pleasure my hope, and praise of Thee my action, and remembrance of Thee my companion, and the power of Thy sovereignty my succorer, and Thy habitation my home, and my dwelling-place the seat Thou hast sanctified from the limitations imposed upon them who are shut out as by a veil from Thee.

Thou art, verily, the Almighty, the All-Glorious, the Most Powerful.

—*Bahá'u'lláh*

4

O Lord! We are weak; strengthen us. O God! We are ignorant; make us knowing. O Lord! We are poor; make us wealthy. O God! We are dead; quicken us. O Lord! We are humiliation itself; glorify us in Thy Kingdom. If Thou dost assist us, O Lord, we shall become as scintillating stars. If Thou dost not assist us, we shall become lower than the earth. O Lord! Strengthen us. O God! Confer victory upon us. O God! Enable us to conquer self and overcome desire. O Lord! Deliver us from the bondage of the material world. O Lord! Quicken us through the breath of the Holy Spirit in order that we may arise to serve Thee, engage in worshiping Thee and exert ourselves in Thy Kingdom with the utmost sincerity. O Lord, Thou art powerful. O God, Thou art forgiving. O Lord, Thou art compassionate.

—'Abdu'l-Bahá

5

O God, my God! Thou art my Hope and my Beloved, my highest Aim and Desire! With great humbleness and entire devotion I pray to Thee to make me a minaret of Thy love in Thy land, a lamp of Thy knowledge among Thy creatures, and a banner of divine bounty in Thy dominion.

Number me with such of Thy servants as have detached themselves from everything but Thee, have sanctified themselves from the transitory things of this world, and have freed themselves from the promptings of the voicers of idle fancies.

Let my heart be dilated with joy through the spirit of confirmation from Thy kingdom, and brighten my eyes by beholding the hosts of divine assistance descending successively upon me from the kingdom of Thine omnipotent glory.

Thou art, in truth, the Almighty, the All-Glorious, the All-Powerful.

—'Abdu'l-Bahá

6

O my God! O my God! Glory be unto Thee for that Thou hast confirmed me to the confession of Thy oneness, attracted me unto the word of Thy singleness, enkindled me by the fire of Thy love, and occupied me with Thy mention and the service of Thy friends and maidservants.

O Lord, help me to be meek and lowly, and strengthen me in severing myself from all things and in holding to the hem of the garment of Thy glory, so that my heart may be filled with Thy love and leave no space for love of the world and attachment to its qualities.

O God! Sanctify me from all else save Thee, purge me from the dross of sins and transgressions, and cause me to possess a spiritual heart and conscience.

Verily, Thou art merciful and, verily, Thou art the Most Generous, Whose help is sought by all men.

—'Abdu'l-Bahá

7

O God, my God! Aid Thou Thy trusted servants to have loving and tender hearts. Help them to spread, amongst all the nations of the earth, the light of guidance that cometh from the Company on high. Verily, Thou art the Strong, the Powerful, the Mighty, the All-

Subduing, the Ever-Giving. Verily, Thou art the Generous, the Gentle, the Tender, the Most Bountiful.

—'Abdu'l-Bahá

❧   ❧   ❧

8

It is only by the breath of the Holy Spirit that spiritual development can come about. No matter how the material world may progress, no matter how splendidly it may adorn itself, it can never be anything but a lifeless body unless the soul is within, for it is the soul that animates the body; the body alone has no real significance. Deprived of the blessings of the Holy Spirit the material body would be inert.

—'Abdu'l-Bahá

9

The laborer cuts up the earth with his plough, and from that earth comes the rich and plentiful harvest. The more a man is chastened, the greater is the harvest of spiritual virtues shown forth by him.

—'Abdu'l-Bahá

10

Let your thoughts dwell on your own spiritual development, and close your eyes to the deficiencies of other souls. Act ye in such wise, showing forth pure and goodly deeds, and modesty and humility, that ye will cause others to be awakened.

—'Abdu'l-Bahá

11

Know, O thou possessors of insight, that true spirituality is like unto a lake of clear water which reflects the divine. Of such was the spirituality of Jesus Christ. There is another kind which is like a mirage, seeming to be spiritual when it is not. That which is truly spiritual must light the path to God, and must result in deeds. We cannot believe the call to be spiritual when there is no result. Spirit is reality, and when the spirit in each of us seeks to join itself with the Great Reality, it must in turn give life.

—'Abdu'l-Bahá

Acquiring Virtues

1

Create in me a pure heart, O my God, and renew a tranquil conscience within me, O my Hope! Through the spirit of power confirm Thou me in Thy Cause, O my Best-Beloved, and by the light of Thy glory reveal unto me Thy path, O Thou the Goal of my desire! Through the power of Thy transcendent might lift me up unto the heaven of Thy holiness, O Source of my being, and by the breezes of Thine eternity gladden me, O Thou Who art my God! Let Thine everlasting melodies breathe tranquillity on me, O my Companion, and let the riches of Thine ancient countenance deliver me from all except Thee, O my Master, and let the tidings of the revelation of Thine incorruptible Essence bring me joy, O Thou Who art the most manifest of the manifest and the most hidden of the hidden!

—*Bahá'u'lláh*

2

I beseech Thee, O my God, by all the tran scendent glory of Thy Name, to clothe Thy loved ones in the robe of justice and to illumine their beings with the light of trustworthiness. Thou art the One Who hath power to do as He pleaseth and Who holdeth within His grasp the reins of all things, visible and invisible.

—*Bahá'u'lláh*

3

O Thou kind Lord! These are Thy servants who have gathered in this meeting, have turned unto Thy kingdom and are in need of Thy bestowal and blessing. O Thou God! Manifest and make evident the signs of Thy oneness which have been deposited in all the realities of life. Reveal and unfold the virtues which Thou hast made latent and concealed in these human realities.

O God! We are as plants, and Thy bounty is as the rain; refresh and cause these plants to grow through Thy bestowal. We are Thy servants; free us from the fetters of material existence. We are ignorant; make us wise. We are dead; make us alive. We are material; endow us with spirit. We are deprived; make us the intimates of Thy mysteries. We are needy; enrich and bless us from Thy boundless treasury. O God! Resuscitate us; give us sight; give us hearing; familiarize us with the mysteries of life, so that the secrets of Thy kingdom may become revealed to us in this world of existence and we may confess Thy oneness. Every bestowal emanates from Thee; every benediction is Thine.

Thou art mighty. Thou art powerful. Thou art the Giver, and Thou art the Ever-Bounteous.

—'Abdu'l-Bahá

4

He is God! O God, my God! Bestow upon me a pure heart, like unto a pearl.

—'Abdu'l-Bahá

ֆ ֆ ֆ

5

All men have been created to carry forward an ever-advancing civilization. The Almighty beareth Me witness: To act like the beasts of the field is unworthy of man. Those virtues that befit his dignity are forbearance, mercy, compassion and loving kindness towards all the peoples and kindreds of the earth.

—Bahá'u'lláh

6

The virtues and attributes pertaining unto God are all evident and manifest, and have been mentioned and described in all the heavenly Books. Among them are trustworthiness, truthfulness, purity of heart while communing with God, forbearance, resignation to whatever the Almighty hath decreed, contentment with the things His Will hath provided, patience, nay, thankfulness in the midst of tribulation, and complete reliance, in all circumstances, upon Him. These rank, according to the estimate of God, among the highest and most laudable of all acts. All other acts are, and will ever remain, secondary and subordinate unto them.

—Bahá'u'lláh

7

Trustworthiness . . . is the door of security for all that dwell on earth and a token of glory on the part of the All-Merciful. He who partaketh thereof hath indeed partaken of the treasures of wealth and prosperity. Trustworthiness is the greatest portal leading unto the tranquillity and security of the people. In truth the stability of every affair hath depended and doth depend upon it. All the domains of power, of grandeur and of wealth are illumined by its light.

—Bahá'u'lláh

8

O friends! Be not careless of the virtues with which ye have been endowed, neither be neglectful of your high destiny. Suffer not your labors to be wasted through the vain imaginations which certain hearts have devised. Ye are the stars of the heaven of understanding, the breeze that stirreth at the break of day, the soft-flowing waters upon which must depend the very life of all men, the letters inscribed upon His sacred scroll. With the utmost unity, and in a spirit of perfect fellowship, exert yourselves, that ye may be enabled to achieve that which beseemeth this Day of God. Verily I say, strife and dissension, and whatsoever the mind of man abhorreth are entirely unworthy of his station.

—Bahá'u'lláh

9

In man there are two natures; his spiritual or higher nature and his material or lower nature. In one he approaches God, in the other he lives for the world alone. Signs of both these natures are to be found in men. In his material aspect he expresses untruth, cruelty and injustice; all these are the outcome of his lower nature. The attributes of his Divine nature are shown forth in love, mercy, kindness, truth and justice, one and all being expressions of his higher nature. Every good habit, every noble quality belongs to man's spiritual nature, whereas all his imperfections and sinful actions are born of his material nature. If a man's Divine nature dominates his human nature, we have a saint.

Man has the power both to do good and to do evil; if his power for good predominates and his inclinations to do wrong are conquered, then man in truth may be called a saint. But if, on the contrary, he rejects the things of God and allows his evil passions to conquer him, then he is no better than a mere animal.

—'Abdu'l-Bahá

10

Verily, it is better a thousand times for a man to die than to continue living without virtue.

We have eyes wherewith to see, but if we do not use them how do they profit us? We have ears wherewith to hear, but if we are deaf of what use are they?

We have a tongue wherewith to praise God and proclaim the good tidings, but if we are dumb how useless it is!

The All-Loving God created man to radiate the Divine light and to illumine the world by his words, action and life. If he is without virtue he becomes no better than a mere animal, and an animal devoid of intelligence is a vile thing.

The Heavenly Father gave the priceless gift of intelligence to man so that he might become a spiritual light, piercing the darkness of materiality, and bringing goodness and truth into the world.

—'Abdu'l-Bahá

11

If the moral precepts and foundations of divine civilization become united with the material advancement of man, there is no doubt that the happiness of the human world will be attained and that from every direction the glad tidings of peace upon earth will be announced. Then humankind will achieve extraordinary progress, the sphere of human intelligence will be immeasurably enlarged, wonderful inventions will appear, and the spirit of God will reveal itself; all men will consort in joy and fragrance, and eternal life will be conferred upon the children of the Kingdom. Then will the power of the divine make itself effective and the breath of the Holy Spirit penetrate the essence of all things. Therefore, the material and the divine, or merciful, civilizations must progress together until the highest aspirations and desires of humanity shall become realized.

—'Abdu'l-Bahá

12

Man must sever himself from the influences of the world of matter, from the world of nature and its laws; for the material world is the world of corruption and death. It is the world of evil and darkness, of animalism and ferocity, bloodthirstiness, ambition and avarice, of self-worship, egotism and passion; it is the world of nature. Man must strip himself of all these imperfections, must sacrifice these tendencies which are peculiar to the outer and material world of existence.

On the other hand, man must acquire heavenly qualities and attain divine attributes. He must become the image and likeness of God. He must seek the bounty of the eternal, become the manifestor of the love of God, the light of guidance, the tree of life and the depository of the bounties of God. That is to say, man must sacrifice the qualities and attributes of the world of nature for the qualities and attributes of the world of God.

—'Abdu'l-Bahá

13

Man is in the highest degree of materiality, and at the beginning of spirituality—that is to say, he is the end of imperfection and the beginning of perfection. He is at the last degree of darkness, and at the beginning of light; that is why it has been said that the condition of man is the end of the night and the beginning of day, meaning that he is the sum of all the degrees of imperfection, and that he possesses the degrees of perfection. He has the animal side as well as the angelic side, and the aim of an educator is to so train human souls that their angelic aspect may overcome their animal side. Then if the divine power in man, which is his essential perfection, overcomes the satanic power, which is absolute imperfection, he becomes the most excellent among the creatures; but if the satanic power overcomes the divine power, he becomes the lowest of the creatures. That is why he is the end of imperfection and the beginning of perfection. Not in any other of the species in the world of existence is there such a difference, contrast, contradiction and opposition as in the species of man.

Knowledge is a quality of man, and so is ignorance; truthfulness is a quality of man; so is falsehood; trustworthiness and treachery, justice and injustice, are qualities of man, and so forth. Briefly, all the perfections and virtues, and all the vices, are qualities of man.

—'Abdu'l-Bahá

14

Truthfulness is the foundation of all the virtues of the world of humanity. Without truthfulness, progress and success in all of the worlds of God are impossible for a soul. When this holy attribute is established in man, all the divine qualities will also become realized.

—'Abdu'l-Bahá

Letting Go of Worldly Matters

1

O God, my God! Thou beholdest me circling round Thy Will with mine eyes turned towards the horizon of Thy bounty, eagerly awaiting the revelation of the effulgent splendors of the sun of Thy favors. I beg of Thee, O Beloved of every understanding heart and the Desire of such as have near access unto Thee, to grant that Thy loved ones may become wholly detached from their own inclinations, holding fast unto that which pleaseth Thee. Attire them, O Lord, with the robe of righteousness and illumine them with the splendors of the light of detachment. Summon then to their assistance the hosts of wisdom and utterance that they may exalt Thy Word amongst Thy creatures and proclaim Thy Cause amidst Thy servants. Verily, potent art Thou to do what Thou willest, and within Thy grasp lie the reins of all affairs. No God is there but Thee, the Mighty, the Ever-Forgiving.

—*Bahá'u'lláh*

2

Exalted art Thou, O Lord my God! I am the one who hath forsaken his all and set his face towards the splendors of the glory of Thy countenance, who hath severed every tie and clung to the cord of Thy love and of Thy good-pleasure. I am he, O my God, who hath embraced Thy love and accepted all the adversities which the world can inflict, who hath offered up himself as a ransom for the sake of Thy loved ones, that they may ascend into the heavens of Thy knowledge and be drawn nearer unto Thee, and may soar in the atmosphere of Thy love and Thy good-pleasure.

Ordain, O my God, for me and for them that which Thou didst decree for such of Thy chosen ones as are wholly devoted unto Thee. Cause them, then, to be numbered among those whose eyes Thou hast cleansed and kept from turning to any one save Thee, and whose eyes Thou hast protected from beholding any face except Thy face.

Thou art, verily, the Almighty, the Most Exalted, the All-Glorious, the Supreme King, the Help in Peril, the All-Pardoner, the Ever-Forgiving.

—Bahá'u'lláh

3

O God, Who art the Author of all Manifestations, the Source of all Sources, the Fountainhead of all Revelations, and the Wellspring of all Lights! I testify that by Thy Name the heaven of understanding hath been adorned, and the ocean of utterance hath surged, and the dispensations of Thy providence have been promulgated unto the followers of all religions.

I beseech Thee so to enrich me as to dispense with all save Thee, and be made independent of anyone except Thyself. Rain down, then, upon me out of the clouds of Thy bounty that which shall profit me in every world of Thy worlds. Assist me, then, through Thy strengthening grace, so to serve Thy Cause amidst Thy servants that I may show forth what will cause me to be remembered as long as Thine own kingdom endureth and Thy dominion will last.

This is Thy servant, O my Lord, who with his whole being hath turned unto the horizon of Thy bounty, and the ocean of Thy grace, and the heaven of Thy gifts. Do with me then as becometh Thy majesty, and Thy glory, and Thy bounteousness, and Thy grace.

Thou, in truth, art the God of strength and power, Who art meet to answer them that pray

Thee. There is no God save Thee, the All-Knowing, the All-Wise.

—*Bahá'u'lláh*

4

Praise be to Thee, O Lord my God! I am the one who hath sought the good pleasure of Thy will, and directed his steps towards the seat of Thy gracious favors. I am he who hath forsaken his all, who hath fled to Thee for shelter, who hath set his face towards the tabernacle of Thy revelation and the adored sanctuary of Thy glory. I beseech Thee, O my Lord, by Thy call whereby they who recognized Thy unity have sought the shadow of Thy most gracious providence, and the sincere have fled far from themselves unto Thy name, the Most Exalted, the All-Glorious, through which Thy verses were sent down, and Thy word fulfilled, and Thy proof manifested, and the sun of Thy beauty risen, and Thy testimony established, and Thy signs uncovered—I beseech Thee to grant that I may be numbered with them that have quaffed the wine that is life indeed from the hands of Thy gracious providence, and have rid themselves, in Thy path, of all attachment to Thy creatures, and been so inebriated with Thy manifold wisdom that they hastened to the field of sacrifice with Thy praise on their lips and Thy remembrance in their hearts. Send down, also, upon me, O my God, that which will wash me from anything that is not of Thee, and deliver me from Thine enemies who have disbelieved in Thy signs.

Potent art Thou to do what Thou willest. No God is there beside Thee, the Help in Peril, the Self-Subsisting.

O my God, my Lord and my Master! I have detached myself from my kindred and have sought through Thee to become independent of all that dwell on earth and ever ready to receive that which is praiseworthy in Thy sight. Bestow on me such good as will make me independent of aught else but Thee, and grant me an ampler share of Thy boundless favors. Verily, Thou art the Lord of grace abounding.

—*Bahá'u'lláh*

5

I implore Thee by the splendor of the light of Thy glorious face, the majesty of Thine ancient grandeur and the power of Thy transcendent sovereignty to ordain for us at this moment every measure of that which is good and seemly and to destine for us every portion of the outpourings of Thy grace. For granting of gifts doth not cause Thee loss, nor doth the bestowing of favors diminish Thy wealth.

Glorified art Thou, O Lord! Verily I am poor while in truth Thou art rich; verily I am lowly while in truth Thou art mighty; verily I am impotent while in truth Thou art powerful; verily I am abased while in truth Thou art the most exalted; verily I am distressed while in truth Thou art the Lord of might.

—The Báb

6

O God, my God! Fill up for me the cup of detachment from all things, and in the assembly of Thy splendors and bestowals, rejoice me with the wine of loving Thee. Free me from the assaults of passion and desire, break off from me the shackles of this nether world, draw me with rapture unto Thy supernal realm, and refresh me amongst the handmaids with the breathings of Thy holiness.

O Lord, brighten Thou my face with the lights of Thy bestowals, light Thou mine eyes with beholding the signs of Thine all-subduing might; delight my heart with the glory of Thy knowledge that encompasseth all things, gladden Thou my soul with Thy soul-reviving tidings of great joy, O Thou King of this world and the Kingdom above, O Thou Lord of dominion and might, that I may spread abroad Thy signs and tokens, and proclaim Thy Cause, and promote Thy Teachings, and serve Thy Law and exalt Thy Word.

Thou art, verily, the Powerful, the Ever-Giving, the Able, the Omnipotent.

—'Abdu'l-Bahá

7

O God, my God! Thou beholdest this weak one begging for celestial strength, this poor one craving Thy heavenly treasures, this thirsty one longing for the fountain of eternal life, this afflicted one yearning for Thy promised healing through Thy boundless mercy which Thou hast destined for Thy chosen servants in Thy kingdom on high.

O Lord! I have no helper save Thee, no shelter besides Thee, and no sustainer except Thee. Assist me with Thine angels to diffuse Thy holy fragrances and to spread abroad Thy teachings amongst the choicest of Thy people.

O my Lord! Suffer me to be detached from aught else save Thee, to hold fast to the hem of Thy bounty, to be wholly devoted to Thy Faith, to remain fast and firm in Thy love and to observe what Thou hast prescribed in Thy Book.

Verily, Thou art the Powerful, the Mighty, the Omnipotent.

—'Abdu'l-Bahá

8

A pure heart is as a mirror; cleanse it with the burnish of love and severance from all save God, that the true sun may shine within it and the eternal morning dawn. Then wilt thou clearly see the meaning of "Neither doth My earth nor My heaven contain Me, but the heart of My faithful servant containeth Me."* And thou wilt take up thy life in thine hand, and with infinite longing cast it before the new Beloved One.

—*Bahá'u'lláh*

9

They that tread the path of faith, they that thirst for the wine of certitude, must cleanse themselves of all that is earthly—their ears from idle talk, their minds from vain imaginings, their hearts from worldly affections, their eyes from that which perisheth. They should put their trust in God, and, holding fast unto Him, follow in His way. Then will they be made worthy of the effulgent glories of the sun of divine

---

* Ḥadíth, i.e., report of an action or utterance traditionally attributed to the Prophet Muḥammad or to one of the holy Imáms.

knowledge and understanding, and become the recipients of a grace that is infinite and unseen, inasmuch as man can never hope to attain unto the knowledge of the All-Glorious, can never quaff from the stream of divine knowledge and wisdom, can never enter the abode of immortality, nor partake of the cup of divine nearness and favor, unless and until he ceases to regard the words and deeds of mortal men as a standard for the true understanding and recognition of God and His Prophets.

—*Bahá'u'lláh*

10

But, O my brother, when a true seeker determineth to take the step of search in the path leading to the knowledge of the Ancient of Days, he must, before all else, cleanse and purify his heart, which is the seat of the revelation of the inner mysteries of God, from the obscuring dust of all acquired knowledge, and the allusions of the embodiments of satanic fancy. He must purge his breast, which is the sanctuary of the abiding love of the Beloved, of every defilement, and sanctify his soul from all that pertaineth to water and clay, from all shadowy and ephemeral attachments. He must so cleanse his heart that no remnant of either love or hate may linger therein, lest that love blindly incline him to error, or that hate repel him away from the truth. Even as thou dost witness in this day how most of the people, because of such love and hate, are bereft of the immortal Face, have strayed far from the Embodiments of the divine mysteries, and, shepherdless, are roaming through the wilderness of oblivion and error. That seeker must at all times put his trust in God, must renounce the peoples of the earth, detach himself from the world of dust, and cleave unto Him Who is the Lord of Lords. He must never seek to exalt himself above any one, must wash away from the tablet of his heart every trace of pride and vainglory, must cling unto patience and resignation, observe silence, and refrain from idle talk. For the tongue is a smoldering fire, and excess of speech a deadly poison. Material fire consumeth the body, whereas the fire of the tongue devoureth both heart and soul. The force of the former lasteth but for a time, whilst the effects of the latter endure a century.

—Bahá'u'lláh

11

Say: O concourse of mirrors! Ye are but creation of My will and have come to exist by virtue of My command. Beware lest ye deny the verses of My Lord, and be of them who have wrought injustice and are numbered with the lost. Beware lest ye cling unto that which ye possess, or take pride in your fame and renown. That which behooveth you is to wholly detach yourselves from all that is in the heavens and on the earth. Thus hath it been ordained by Him Who is the All-Powerful, the Almighty.

—*Bahá'u'lláh*

12

We must look higher than all earthly thoughts; detach ourselves from every material idea, crave for the things of the spirit; fix our eyes on the everlasting bountiful Mercy of the Almighty, who will fill our souls with the gladness of joyful service to His command "Love One Another."

—*'Abdu'l-Bahá*

Drawing Closer to God

1

Lauded and glorified art Thou, O my God! I entreat Thee by the sighing of Thy lovers and by the tears shed by them that long to behold Thee, not to withhold from me Thy tender mercies in Thy Day, nor to deprive me of the melodies of the Dove that extolleth Thy oneness before the light that shineth from Thy face. I am the one who is in misery, O God! Behold me cleaving fast to Thy Name, the All-Possessing. I am the one who is sure to perish; behold me clinging to Thy Name, the Imperishable. I implore Thee, therefore, by Thy Self, the Exalted, the Most High, not to abandon me unto mine own self and unto the desires of a corrupt inclination. Hold Thou my hand with the hand of Thy power, and deliver me from the depths of my fancies and idle imaginings, and cleanse me of all that is abhorrent unto Thee.

Cause me, then, to turn wholly unto Thee, to put my whole trust in Thee, to seek Thee as my Refuge, and to flee unto Thy face. Thou art, verily, He Who, through the power of His might, doeth whatsoever He desireth, and commandeth, through the potency of His will, whatsoever He chooseth. None can withstand the operation of

Thy decree; none can divert the course of Thine appointment. Thou art, in truth, the Almighty, the All-Glorious, the Most Bountiful.

—*Bahá'u'lláh*

2

Suffer me, O my God, to draw nigh unto Thee, and to abide within the precincts of Thy court, for remoteness from Thee hath well-nigh consumed me. Cause me to rest under the shadow of the wings of Thy grace, for the flame of my separation from Thee hath melted my heart within me. Draw me nearer unto the river that is life indeed, for my soul burneth with thirst in its ceaseless search after Thee. My sighs, O my God, proclaim the bitterness of mine anguish, and the tears I shed attest my love for Thee.

I beseech Thee, by the praise wherewith Thou praisest Thyself and the glory wherewith Thou glorifiest Thine own Essence, to grant that we may be numbered among them that have recognized Thee and acknowledged Thy sovereignty in Thy days. Help us then to quaff, O my God, from the fingers of mercy the living waters of Thy loving-kindness, that we may utterly forget all else except Thee, and be occupied only with Thy Self. Powerful art Thou to do what Thou willest. No God is there beside Thee, the Mighty, the Help in Peril, the Self-Subsisting.

Glorified be Thy name, O Thou Who art the King of all Kings!

—*Bahá'u'lláh*

3

O Thou Whose face is the object of the adoration of all that yearn after Thee, Whose presence is the hope of such as are wholly devoted to Thy will, Whose nearness is the desire of all that have drawn nigh unto Thy court, Whose countenance is the companion of those who have recognized Thy truth, Whose name is the mover of the souls that long to behold Thy face, Whose voice is the true life of Thy lovers, the words of Whose mouth are as the waters of life unto all who are in heaven and on earth!

I beseech Thee, by the wrong Thou hast suffered and the ills inflicted upon Thee by the hosts of wrongful doers, to send down upon me from the clouds of Thy mercy that which will purify me of all that is not of Thee, that I may be worthy to praise Thee and fit to love Thee.

Withhold not from me, O my Lord, the things Thou didst ordain for such of Thy handmaidens as circle around Thee, and on whom are poured continually the splendors of the sun of Thy beauty and the beams of the brightness of Thy face. Thou art He Who from everlasting hath succored whosoever hath sought Thee, and bountifully favored him who hath asked Thee.

No God is there beside Thee, the Mighty, the Ever-Abiding, the All-Bounteous, the Most Generous.

—Bahá'u'lláh

4

Many a chilled heart, O my God, hath been set ablaze with the fire of Thy Cause, and many a slumberer hath been wakened by the sweetness of Thy voice. How many are the strangers who have sought shelter beneath the shadow of the tree of Thy oneness, and how numerous the thirsty ones who have panted after the fountain of Thy living waters in Thy days!

Blessed is he that hath set himself towards Thee, and hasted to attain the Dayspring of the lights of Thy face. Blessed is he who with all his affections hath turned to the Dawning-Place of Thy Revelation and the Fountainhead of Thine inspiration. Blessed is he that hath expended in Thy path what Thou didst bestow upon him through Thy bounty and favor. Blessed is he who, in his sore longing after Thee, hath cast away all else except Thyself. Blessed is he who hath enjoyed intimate communion with Thee, and rid himself of all attachment to anyone save Thee.

I beseech Thee, O my Lord, by Him Who is Thy Name, Who, through the power of Thy sovereignty and might, hath risen above the horizon of His prison, to ordain for everyone what becometh Thee and beseemeth Thine exaltation.

Thy might, in truth, is equal to all things.

—*Bahá'u'lláh*

5

Verily I am Thy servant, O my God, and Thy poor one and Thy suppliant and Thy wretched creature. I have arrived at Thy gate, seeking Thy shelter. I have found no contentment save in Thy love, no exultation except in Thy remembrance, no eagerness but in obedience to Thee, no joy save in Thy nearness, and no tranquillity except in reunion with Thee, notwithstanding that I am conscious that all created things are debarred from Thy sublime Essence and the entire creation is denied access to Thine inmost Being. Whenever I attempt to approach Thee, I perceive nothing in myself but the tokens of Thy grace and behold naught in my being but the revelations of Thy loving-kindness. How can one who is but Thy creature seek reunion with Thee and attain unto Thy presence, whereas no created thing can ever be associated with Thee, nor can aught comprehend Thee? How is it possible for a lowly servant to recognize Thee and to extol Thy praise, notwithstanding that Thou hast destined for him the revelations of Thy dominion and the wondrous testimonies of Thy sovereignty? Thus every created thing beareth witness that it is debarred from the sanctuary of Thy presence by reason of the limitations imposed upon its inner reality. It is undisputed, however, that the influence of Thine attraction hath everlastingly been inherent in the realities of Thy handiwork, although that which beseemeth the hallowed court of Thy providence is exalted beyond the attainment of the entire creation. This indicateth, O my God, my utter powerlessness to praise Thee and revealeth my utmost impotence in yielding thanks unto Thee; and how much more to attain the recognition of Thy divine unity or to succeed in reaching the clear tokens of Thy praise, Thy sanctity and Thy glory. Nay, by Thy might, I yearn for naught but Thine Own Self and seek no one other than Thee.

—*The Báb*

6

Praised and glorified art Thou, O God! Grant that the day of attaining Thy holy presence may be fast approaching. Cheer our hearts through the potency of Thy love and good-pleasure, and bestow upon us steadfastness that we may willingly submit to Thy Will and Thy Decree. Verily, Thy knowledge embraceth all the things Thou hast created or wilt create, and Thy celestial might transcendeth whatsoever Thou hast called or wilt call into being. There is none to be worshiped but Thee, there is none to be desired except Thee, there is none to be adored besides Thee and there is naught to be loved save Thy good-pleasure.

Verily, Thou art the supreme Ruler, the Sovereign Truth, the Help in Peril, the Self-Subsisting.

—*The Báb*

7

Thou art God, no God is there but Thee.

Lauded and glorified art Thou, O Lord my God! Thou art supreme over the realm of being and Thy power pervadeth all created things. Thou holdest the kingdom of creation within Thy grasp and dost call into being in conformity with Thy pleasure.

All praise be unto Thee, O Lord my God! I beseech Thee by such souls as are eagerly waiting at Thy gate and by those holy beings who have attained the court of Thy presence, to cast upon us the glances of Thy tender compassion and to regard us with the eye of Thy loving providence.

Cause our souls to be enkindled with the fire of Thy tender affection and give us to drink of the living waters of Thy bounty. Keep us steadfast in the path of Thine ardent love and enable us to abide within the precincts of Thy holiness. Verily Thou art the Giver, the Most Generous, the All-Knowing, the All-Informed.

Glorified art Thou, O my God! I invoke Thee by Thy Most Great Name through which the hidden secrets of God, the Most Exalted, were divulged and the kindreds of all nations converged toward the focal centre of faith and certitude, through which Thy luminous Words streamed forth for the quickening of mankind and the essence of all knowledge was revealed from that Embodiment of bounty. May my life, my inmost being, my soul and my body be offered up as a sacrifice for the dust ennobled by His footsteps.

I earnestly beg Thee, O Lord my God, by Thy most glorious Name whereby Thy sovereignty hath been established and the tokens of Thy might have been manifested, and whereby the oceans of life and of holy ecstasy have surged for the reviving of the moldering bones of all Thy creatures and for the stirring of the limbs of such as have embraced Thy Cause—I earnestly beg Thee to graciously ordain for us the good of this world and of the next, to enable us to gain admission into the court of Thy mercy and loving-kindness and to kindle in our hearts the fire of joy and ecstasy in such wise that the hearts of all men may thereby be attracted.

Verily Thou art the All-Powerful, the Protector, the Almighty, the Self-Subsisting.

—*The Báb*

8

O God, my God! This is Thy radiant servant, Thy spiritual thrall, who hath drawn nigh unto Thee and approached Thy presence. He hath turned his face unto Thine, acknowledging Thy oneness, confessing Thy singleness, and he hath called out in Thy name among the nations, and led the people to the streaming waters of Thy mercy, O Thou Most generous Lord! To those who asked He hath given to drink from the cup of guidance that brimmeth over with the wine of Thy measureless grace.

O Lord, assist him under all conditions, cause him to learn Thy well-guarded mysteries, and shower down upon him Thy hidden pearls. Make of him a banner rippling from castle summits in the winds of Thy heavenly aid, make of him a wellspring of crystal waters.

O my forgiving Lord! Light up the hearts with the rays of a lamp that sheddeth abroad its beams, disclosing to those among Thy people whom Thou hast bounteously favored, the realities of all things.

Verily, Thou art the Mighty, the Powerful, the Protector, the Strong, the Beneficent! Verily, Thou art the Lord of all mercies!

—'Abdu'l-Bahá

ও   ও   ও

9

O Son of Being! Thy Paradise is My love; thy heavenly home, reunion with Me. Enter therein and tarry not. This is that which hath been destined for thee in Our kingdom above and Our exalted dominion.

— Bahá'u'lláh

10

Where is he to be found who, through the power of My name that transcendeth all created things, will cast away the things that men possess, and cling, with all his might, to the things which God, the Knower of the unseen and of the seen, hath bidden him observe? Thus hath His bounty been sent down unto men, His testimony fulfilled, and His proof shone forth above the Horizon of mercy. Rich is the prize that shall be won by him who hath believed and exclaimed: "Lauded art Thou, O Beloved of all worlds! Magnified be Thy name, O Thou the Desire of every understanding heart!"

—Bahá'u'lláh

11

He Who is the Dayspring of Truth is, no doubt, fully capable of rescuing from such remoteness wayward souls and of causing them to draw nigh unto His court and attain His Presence. "If God had pleased He had surely made all men one people." His purpose, however, is to enable the pure in spirit and the detached in heart to ascend, by virtue of their own innate powers, unto the shores of the Most Great Ocean, that thereby they who seek the Beauty of the All-Glorious may be distinguished and separated from the wayward and perverse. Thus hath it been ordained by the all-glorious and resplendent Pen.

—Bahá'u'lláh

12

Divine nearness is dependent upon attainment to the knowledge of God, upon severance from all else save God. It is contingent upon self-sacrifice and to be found only through forfeiting wealth and worldly possessions. It is made possible through the baptism of water and fire revealed in the Gospels. Water symbolizes the water of life, which is knowledge, and fire is the fire of the love of God; therefore, man must be baptized with the water of life, the Holy Spirit and the fire of the love of the Kingdom. Until he attains these three degrees, nearness to God is not possible. . . . And be it known that this nearness is not dependent upon time or place. Nearness to God is dependent upon purity of the heart and exhilaration of the spirit through the glad tidings of the Kingdom. Consider how a pure, well-polished mirror fully reflects the effulgence of the sun, no matter how distant the sun may be. As soon as the mirror is cleaned and purified, the sun will manifest itself. The more pure and sanctified the heart of man becomes, the nearer it draws to God, and the light of the Sun of Reality is revealed within it. This light sets hearts aglow with the fire of the love of God, opens in them the doors of knowledge and unseals the divine mysteries so that spiritual discoveries are made possible. All the Prophets have drawn near to God through severance. We must emulate those Holy Souls and renounce our own wishes and desires. We must purify ourselves from the mire and soil of earthly contact until our hearts become as mirrors in clearness and the light of the most great guidance reveals itself in them.

—'Abdu'l-Bahá

Steadfastness

1

I implore Thee, O my God and my Master, by Thy word through which they who have believed in Thy unity have soared up into the atmosphere of Thy knowledge, and they who are devoted to Thee have ascended into the heaven of Thy oneness, to inspire Thy loved ones with that which will assure their hearts in Thy Cause. Endue them with such steadfastness that nothing whatsoever will hinder them from turning towards Thee.

Thou art, verily, the Bountiful, the Munificent, the Forgiving, the Compassionate.

—*Bahá'u'lláh*

2

Glorified be Thy name, O Lord my God! I beseech Thee by Thy power that hath encompassed all created things, and by Thy Sovereignty that hath transcended the entire creation, and by Thy Word which was hidden in Thy wisdom and whereby Thou didst create Thy heaven and Thy earth, both to enable us to be steadfast in our love for Thee and in our obedience to Thy pleasure, and to fix our gaze upon Thy face, and celebrate Thy glory. Empower us, then, O my God, to spread abroad Thy signs among Thy creatures, and to guard Thy Faith in Thy realm. Thou hast ever existed independently of the mention of any of Thy creatures, and wilt remain as Thou hast been for ever and ever.

In Thee I have placed my whole confidence, unto Thee I have turned my face, to the cord of Thy loving providence I have clung, and towards the shadow of Thy mercy I have hastened. Cast me not as one disappointed out of Thy door, O my God, and withhold not from me Thy grace, for Thee alone do I seek. No God is there beside Thee, the Ever-Forgiving, the Most Bountiful.

Praise be to Thee, O Thou Who art the Beloved of them that have known Thee!

—*Bahá'u'lláh*

3

O God, my God! I have turned in repentance unto Thee, and verily Thou art the Pardoner, the Compassionate.

O God, my God! I have returned to Thee, and verily Thou art the Ever-Forgiving, the Gracious.

O God, my God! I have clung to the cord of Thy bounty, and with Thee is the storehouse of all that is in heaven and earth.

O God, my God! I have hastened toward Thee, and verily Thou art the Forgiver, the Lord of grace abounding.

O God, my God! I thirst for the celestial wine of Thy grace, and verily Thou art the Giver, the Bountiful, the Gracious, the Almighty.

O God, my God! I testify that Thou hast revealed Thy Cause, fulfilled Thy promise and sent down from the heaven of Thy grace that which hath drawn unto Thee the hearts of Thy favored ones. Well is it with him that hath held fast unto Thy firm cord and clung to the hem of Thy resplendent robe!

I ask Thee, O Lord of all being and King of the seen and unseen, by Thy power, Thy majesty and Thy sovereignty, to grant that my name may be recorded by Thy pen of glory among Thy devoted ones, them whom the scrolls of the sinful hindered not from turning to the light of Thy countenance, O prayer-hearing, prayer-answering God!

—*Bahá'u'lláh*

4

Unto Thee be praise, O Lord my God! I testify that Thou art God, and that there is none other God besides Thee. Thou hast from eternity been immeasurably exalted above the praise of any one except Thee, and far above the description of any of Thy creatures. All created things have borne witness to Thy unity, and every dweller in Thy kingdom hath confessed Thy oneness. The essence of the apprehension of the assured among Thy creatures can never attain unto Thee, and the gem-like utterances with which Thy people have praised and glorified Thee can never hope to ascend unto the atmosphere of Thy holiness. For men's apprehension of Thee is but the apprehension of Thine own creation; how can it reach up to Thee? And all human praise and glorification of Thee pertain unto Thy servants; how can they be deemed worthy of the court of Thy oneness?

I swear by Thy glory! The quintessence of knowledge is powerless to comprehend Thy nature, and the inmost reality of every praise of Thee falleth short of the seat of Thy great glory and of Thine all-compelling power. Every utterance that seeketh to describe Thee, and every knowledge that attempteth to comprehend Thee, is but an expression of Thine own creating, and is begotten by Thy will, and fashioned in conformity with Thy purpose.

I implore Thee, O Thou Who art inscrutable to all except Thee, and can be comprehended through naught else save Thyself, by the wrongs which He Who is the Dayspring of Thy Cause hath suffered at the hands of the ignoble among Thy creatures, and by what hath befallen Him in Thy path, to grant that I may, at all times, be wholly dissolved in Thee, and fix my gaze upon the horizon of Thy will and be steadfast in Thy love.

I have, O my Lord, turned unto Thee according to what Thou hast commanded me in Thy Book, and have set my face towards the horizon of Thy loving-kindness even as Thou hast permitted me in Thy Tablets. Cast me not out of the door of Thy grace, I beseech Thee, and write down for me the recompense destined for him who hath entered Thy presence, and hath risen to serve Thee, and hath been carried away by the drops sprinkled upon him from the Ocean of Thy favors in Thy days, and by the splendors of the Day-Star of Thy gifts that have been shed upon him at the revelation of the light of Thy countenance.

Potent art Thou to do what pleaseth Thee. No God is there save Thee, the Help in Peril, the Self-Subsisting.

—*Bahá'u'lláh*

5

Lauded be Thy Name, O Lord our God! Thou art in truth the Knower of things unseen. Ordain for us such good as Thine all-embracing knowledge can measure. Thou art the sovereign Lord, the Almighty, the Best-Beloved.

All praise be unto Thee, O Lord! We shall seek Thy grace on the appointed Day and shall put our whole reliance in Thee, Who art our Lord. Glorified art Thou, O God! Grant us that which is good and seemly that we may be able to dispense with everything but Thee. Verily, Thou art the Lord of all worlds.

O God! Recompense those who endure patiently in Thy days, and strengthen their hearts to walk undeviatingly in the path of Truth. Grant then, O Lord, such goodly gifts as would enable them to gain admittance into Thy blissful Paradise. Exalted art Thou, O Lord God. Let Thy heavenly blessings descend upon homes whose inmates have believed in Thee. Verily, unsurpassed art Thou in sending down divine blessings. Send forth, O God, such hosts as would render Thy faithful servants victorious. Thou dost fashion the created things through the power of Thy decree as Thou pleasest. Thou art in truth the Sovereign, the Creator, the All-Wise.

Say: God is indeed the Maker of all things. He giveth sustenance in plenty to whomsoever He willeth. He is the Creator, the Source of all beings, the Fashioner, the Almighty, the Maker, the All-Wise. He is the Bearer of the most excellent titles throughout the heavens and the earth and whatever lieth between them. All do His bidding, and all the dwellers of earth and heaven celebrate His praise, and unto Him shall all return.

—*The Báb*

6

Make firm our steps, O Lord, in Thy path and strengthen Thou our hearts in Thine obedience. Turn our faces toward the beauty of Thy oneness, and gladden our bosoms with the signs of Thy divine unity. Adorn our bodies with the robe of Thy bounty, and remove from our eyes the veil of sinfulness, and give us the chalice of Thy grace; that the essence of all beings may sing Thy praise before the vision of Thy grandeur. Reveal then Thyself, O Lord, by Thy merciful utterance and the mystery of Thy divine being, that the holy ecstasy of prayer may fill our souls—a prayer that shall rise above words and letters and transcend the murmur of syllables and sounds—that all things may be merged into nothingness before the revelation of Thy splendor.

Lord! These are servants that have remained fast and firm in Thy Covenant and Thy Testament, that have held fast unto the cord of constancy in Thy Cause and clung unto the hem of the robe of Thy grandeur. Assist them, O Lord, with Thy grace, confirm with Thy power and strengthen their loins in obedience to Thee.

Thou art the Pardoner, the Gracious.

—'Abdu'l-Bahá

7

O my God! O my God! This, Thy servant, hath advanced towards Thee, is passionately wandering in the desert of Thy love, walking in the path of Thy service, anticipating Thy favors, hoping for Thy bounty, relying upon Thy kingdom, and intoxicated by the wine of Thy gift. O my God! Increase the fervor of his affection for Thee, the constancy of his praise of Thee, and the ardor of his love for Thee.

Verily, Thou art the Most Generous, the Lord of grace abounding. There is no other God but Thee, the Forgiving, the Merciful.

—*'Abdu'l-Bahá*

❧   ❧   ❧

8

The spirit that animateth the human heart is the knowledge of God, and its truest adorning is the recognition of the truth that "He doeth whatsoever He willeth, and ordaineth that which He pleaseth." Its raiment is the fear of God, and its perfection steadfastness in His Faith. Thus God instructeth whosoever seeketh Him. He, verily, loveth the one that turneth towards Him. There is none other God but Him, the Forgiving, the Most Bountiful. All praise be to God, the Lord of all worlds.

—*Bahá'u'lláh*

9

Blessed is the man that hath turned his face towards God, and walked steadfastly in His love, until his soul hath winged its flight unto God, the Sovereign Lord of all, the Most Powerful, the Ever-Forgiving, the All-Merciful.

— *Bahá'u'lláh*

10

We cherish the hope that men of piety may illumine the world through the radiant light of their conduct, and We entreat the Almighty—glorified and exalted is He—to grant that everyone may in this Day remain steadfast in His love and stand firm in His Cause. He is, in truth, the Protector of those who are wholly devoted to Him and observe His precepts.

—*Bahá'u'lláh*

11

The beloved of the Lord must stand fixed as the mountains, firm as impregnable walls. Unmoved must they remain by even the direst adversities, ungrieved by the worst of disasters. Let them cling to the hem of Almighty God, and put their faith in the Beauty of the Most High; let them lean on the unfailing help that cometh from the Ancient Kingdom, and depend on the care and protection of the generous

Lord. Let them at all times refresh and restore themselves with the dews of heavenly grace, and with the breaths of the Holy Spirit revive and renew themselves from moment to moment. Let them rise up to serve their Lord, and do all in their power to scatter His breathings of holiness far and wide.

—*'Abdu'l-Bahá*

Healing

1

O God, my God! I beg of Thee by the ocean of Thy healing, and by the splendors of the Daystar of Thy grace, and by Thy Name through which Thou didst subdue Thy servants, and by the pervasive power of Thy most exalted Word and the potency of Thy most august Pen, and by Thy mercy that hath preceded the creation of all who are in heaven and on earth, to purge me with the waters of Thy bounty from every affliction and disorder, and from all weakness and feebleness.

Thou seest, O my Lord, Thy suppliant waiting at the door of Thy bounty, and him who hath set his hopes on Thee clinging to the cord of Thy generosity. Deny him not, I beseech Thee, the things he seeketh from the ocean of Thy grace and the Daystar of Thy loving-kindness.

Powerful art Thou to do what pleaseth Thee. There is none other God save Thee, the Ever-Forgiving, the Most Generous.

—*Bahá'u'lláh*

2

Thy name is my healing, O my God, and remembrance of Thee is my remedy. Near-

143

ness to Thee is my hope, and love for Thee is my companion. Thy mercy to me is my healing and my succor in both this world and the world to come. Thou, verily, art the All-Bountiful, the All-Knowing, the All-Wise.

—*Bahá'u'lláh*

3

Glory be to Thee, O Lord my God! I implore Thee by Thy Name, through which Thou didst lift up the ensigns of Thy guidance, and didst shed the radiance of Thy loving-kindness, and didst reveal the sovereignty of Thy Lordship; through which the lamp of Thy names hath appeared within the niche of Thine attributes, and He Who is the Tabernacle of Thy unity and the Manifestation of detachment hath shone forth; through which the ways of Thy guidance were made known, and the paths of Thy good pleasure were marked out; through which the foundations of error have been made to tremble, and the signs of wickedness have been abolished; through which the fountains of wisdom have burst forth, and the heavenly table hath been sent down; through which Thou didst preserve Thy servants and didst vouchsafe Thy healing; through which Thou didst show forth Thy tender mercies unto Thy servants and revealedst Thy forgiveness amidst Thy creatures—I implore Thee to keep safe him who hath held fast and returned unto Thee, and clung to Thy mercy, and seized the hem of Thy loving providence. Send down, then, upon him Thy healing, and make him whole, and endue him with a constancy vouchsafed by Thee, and a tranquillity bestowed by Thy highness.

Thou art, verily, the Healer, the Preserver, the Helper, the Almighty, the Powerful, the All-Glorious, the All-Knowing.

—Bahá'u'lláh

4

Praised be Thou, O Lord my God! I implore Thee, by Thy Most Great Name through which Thou didst stir up Thy servants and build up Thy cities, and by Thy most excellent titles, and Thy most august attributes, to assist Thy people to turn in the direction of Thy manifold bounties, and set their faces towards the Tabernacle of Thy wisdom. Heal Thou the sicknesses that have assailed the souls on every side, and have deterred them from directing their gaze towards the Paradise that lieth in the shelter of Thy shadowing Name, which Thou didst ordain to be the King of all names unto all who are in heaven and all who are on earth.

Potent art Thou to do as pleaseth Thee. In Thy hands is the empire of all names. There is none other God but Thee, the Mighty, the Wise.

I am but a poor creature, O my Lord; I have clung to the hem of Thy riches. I am sore sick; I have held fast the cord of Thy healing. Deliver me from the ills that have encircled me, and wash me thoroughly with the waters of Thy graciousness and mercy, and attire me with the raiment of wholesomeness, through Thy forgiveness and bounty. Fix, then, mine eyes upon Thee, and rid me of all attachment to aught else except Thyself. Aid me to do what Thou desirest, and to fulfill what Thou pleasest.

Thou art truly the Lord of this life and of the next. Thou art, in truth, the Ever-Forgiving, the Most Merciful.

—Bahá'u'lláh

5

Praise be to Thee, O Lord my God, my Master! Thou hearest the sighing of those who, though they long to behold Thy face, are yet separated from Thee and far distant from Thy court. Thou testifiest to the lamentations which those who have recognized Thee pour forth because of their exile from Thee and their yearning to meet Thee. I beseech Thee by those hearts which contain naught except the treasures of

Thy remembrance and praise, and which show forth only the testimonies of Thy greatness and the evidences of Thy might, to bestow on Thy servants who desire Thee power to approach the seat of the revelation of the splendor of Thy glory and to assist them whose hopes are set on Thee to enter into the tabernacle of Thy transcendent favor and mercy.

Naked am I, O my God! Clothe me with the robe of Thy tender mercies. I am sore athirst; give me to drink of the oceans of Thy bountiful favor. I am a stranger; draw me nearer unto the source of Thy gifts. I am sick; sprinkle upon me the healing waters of Thy grace. I am a captive; rid me of my bondage, by the power of Thy might and through the force of Thy will, that I may soar on the wings of detachment towards the loftiest summits of Thy creation. Thou, verily, doest what Thou choosest. There is no God but Thee, the Help in Peril, the All-Glorious, the Unconstrained.

—*Bahá'u'lláh*

For Women

6

Glory be to Thee, O Lord my God! I beg of Thee by Thy Name through which He Who is Thy Beauty hath been stablished upon the throne of Thy Cause, and by Thy Name through which Thou changest all things, and gatherest together all things, and callest to account all things, and rewardest all things, and preservest all things, and sustainest all things—I beg of Thee to guard this handmaiden who hath fled for refuge to Thee, and hath sought the shelter of Him in Whom Thou Thyself art manifest, and hath put her whole trust and confidence in Thee.

She is sick, O my God, and hath entered beneath the shadow of the Tree of Thy healing; afflicted, and hath fled to the City of Thy protection; diseased, and hath sought the Fountainhead of Thy favors; sorely vexed, and hath hasted to attain the Wellspring of Thy tranquillity; burdened with sin, and hath set her face toward the court of Thy forgiveness.

Attire her, by Thy sovereignty and Thy lovingkindness, O my God and my Beloved, with the raiment of Thy balm and Thy healing, and make her quaff of the cup of Thy mercy and Thy favors. Protect her, moreover, from every affliction and ailment, from all pain and sickness, and from whatsoever may be abhorrent unto Thee.

Thou, in truth, art immensely exalted above all else except Thyself. Thou art, verily, the Healer, the All-Sufficing, the Preserver, the Ever-Forgiving, the Most Merciful.

—*Bahá'u'lláh*

For Infants

7

Thou art He, O my God, through Whose names the sick are healed and the ailing are restored, and thirsty given drink and the sore vexed are tranquilized, and the wayward are guided, and the abased are exalted, and the poor are enriched, and the ignorant are enlightened, and the gloomy are illumined, and the sorrowful are cheered, and the chilled are warmed, and the downtrodden are raised up. Through Thy name, O my God, all created things were stirred up, and the heavens were spread, and the earth was established, and the clouds were raised and made to rain upon the earth. This, verily, is a token of Thy grace unto all Thy creatures.

I implore Thee, therefore, by Thy name through which Thou didst manifest Thy Godhead, and didst exalt Thy Cause above all creation, and by each of Thy most excellent titles and most august attributes, and by all the virtues wherewith Thy transcendent and most exalted Being is extolled, to send down this night from the clouds of Thy mercy the rains of Thy healing upon this suckling, whom Thou hast related unto Thine all-glorious Self in the kingdom of Thy creation. Clothe him, then, O my God, by Thy grace, with the robe of well-being and health, and guard him, O my Beloved, from every affliction and disorder, and from whatsoever is obnoxious unto Thee. Thy might, verily, is equal to all things. Thou, in truth, art the Most Powerful, the Self-Subsisting. Send down, moreover, upon him, O my God, the good of this world and of the next, and the good of the former and latter generations. Thy might and Thy wisdom are, verily, equal unto this.

—Bahá'u'lláh

The Long Healing Prayer
8

He is the Healer, the Sufficer, the Helper, the All-Forgiving, the All-Merciful.

I call on Thee O Exalted One, O Faithful One, O Glorious One! Thou the Sufficing, Thou the Healing, Thou the Abiding, O Thou Abiding One!

I call on Thee O Sovereign, O Upraiser, O Judge! Thou the Sufficing, Thou the Healing, Thou the Abiding, O Thou Abiding One!

I call on Thee O Peerless One, O Eternal One, O Single One! Thou the Sufficing, Thou the Healing, Thou the Abiding, O Thou Abiding One!

I call on Thee O Most Praised One, O Holy One, O Helping One! Thou the Sufficing, thou the Healing, Thou the Abiding, O Thou Abiding One!

I call on Thee O Omniscient, O Most Wise, O Most Great One! Thou the Sufficing, Thou the Healing, Thou the Abiding, O Thou Abiding One!

I call on Thee O Clement One, O Majestic One, O Ordaining One! Thou the Sufficing, Thou the Healing, Thou the Abiding, O Thou Abiding One!

I call on Thee O Beloved One, O Cherished One, O Enraptured One! Thou the Sufficing, Thou the Healing, Thou the Abiding, O Thou Abiding One!

I call on Thee O Mightiest One, O Sustaining One, O Potent One! Thou the Sufficing, Thou the Healing, Thou the Abiding, O Thou Abiding One!

I call on Thee O Ruling One, O Self-Subsisting, O All-Knowing One! Thou the Sufficing, Thou the Healing, Thou the Abiding, O Thou Abiding One!

I call on Thee O Spirit, O Light, O Most Manifest One! Thou the Sufficing, Thou the Healing, Thou the Abiding, O Thou Abiding One!

I call on Thee O Thou Frequented by all, O Thou Known to all, O Thou Hidden from all! Thou the Sufficing, Thou the Healing, Thou the Abiding, O Thou Abiding One!

I call on Thee O Concealed One, O Triumphant One, O Bestowing One! Thou the Sufficing, Thou the Healing, Thou the Abiding, O Thou Abiding One!

I call on Thee O Almighty, O Succoring One, O Concealing One! Thou the Sufficing, Thou the Healing, Thou the Abiding, O Thou Abiding One!

I call on Thee O Fashioner, O Satisfier, O Uprooter! Thou the Sufficing, Thou the Healing, Thou the Abiding, O Thou Abiding One!

I call on Thee O Rising One, O Gathering One, O Exalting One! Thou the Sufficing, Thou the Healing, Thou the Abiding, O Thou Abiding One!

I call on Thee O Perfecting One, O Unfettered One, O Bountiful One! Thou the Sufficing, Thou the Healing, Thou the Abiding, O Thou Abiding One!

I call on Thee O Beneficent One, O Withholding One, O Creating One! Thou the Sufficing, Thou the Healing, Thou the Abiding, O Thou Abiding One!

I call on Thee O Most Sublime One, O Beauteous One, O Bounteous One! Thou the Sufficing, Thou the Healing, Thou the Abiding, O Thou Abiding One!

I call on Thee O Just One, O Gracious One, O Generous One! Thou the Sufficing, Thou the

Healing, Thou the Abiding, O Thou Abiding One!

I call on Thee O All-Compelling, O Ever-Abiding, O Most Knowing One! Thou the Sufficing, Thou the Healing, Thou the Abiding, O Thou Abiding One!

I call on Thee O Magnificent One, O Ancient of Days, O Magnanimous One! Thou the Sufficing, Thou the Healing, Thou the Abiding, O Thou Abiding One!

I call on Thee O Well-Guarded One, O Lord of Joy, O Desired One! Thou the Sufficing, Thou the Healing, Thou the Abiding, O Thou Abiding One!

I call on Thee O Thou Kind to all, O Thou Compassionate with all, O Most Benevolent One! Thou the Sufficing, Thou the Healing, Thou the Abiding, O Thou Abiding One!

I call on Thee O Haven for all, O Shelter to all, O All-Preserving One! Thou the Sufficing, Thou the Healing, Thou the Abiding, O Thou Abiding One!

I call on Thee O Thou Succorer of all, O Thou Invoked by all, O Quickening One! Thou the Sufficing, Thou the Healing, Thou the Abiding, O Thou Abiding One!

I call on Thee O Unfolder, O Ravager, O Most Clement One! Thou the Sufficing, Thou the Healing, Thou the Abiding, O Thou Abiding One!

I call on Thee O Thou my Soul, O Thou my Beloved, O Thou my Faith! Thou the Sufficing, Thou the Healing, Thou the Abiding, O Thou Abiding One!

I call on Thee O Quencher of thirsts, O Transcendent Lord, O Most Precious One! Thou the Sufficing, Thou the Healing, Thou the Abiding, O Thou Abiding One!

I call on Thee O Greatest Remembrance, O Noblest Name, O Most Ancient Way! Thou the Sufficing, Thou the Healing, Thou the Abiding, O Thou Abiding One!

I call on Thee O Most Lauded, O Most Holy, O Sanctified One! Thou the Sufficing, Thou the Healing, Thou the Abiding, O Thou Abiding One!

I call on Thee O Unfastener, O Counselor, O Deliverer! Thou the Sufficing, Thou the Healing, Thou the Abiding, O Thou Abiding One!

I call on Thee O Friend, O Physician, O Captivating One! Thou the Sufficing, Thou the Healing, Thou the Abiding, O Thou Abiding One!

I call on Thee O Glory, O Beauty, O Bountiful One! Thou the Sufficing, Thou the Healing, Thou the Abiding, O Thou Abiding One!

I call on Thee O the Most Trusted, O the Best Lover, O Lord of the Dawn! Thou the Sufficing, Thou the Healing, Thou the Abiding, O Thou Abiding One!

I call on Thee O Enkindler, O Brightener, O Bringer of Delight! Thou the Sufficing, Thou the Healing, Thou the Abiding, O Thou Abiding One!

I call on Thee O Lord of Bounty, O Most Compassionate, O Most Merciful One! Thou the Sufficing, Thou the Healing, Thou the Abiding, O Thou Abiding One!

I call on Thee O Constant One, O Life-Giving One, O Source of all Being! Thou the Sufficing, Thou the Healing, Thou the Abiding, O Thou Abiding One!

I call on Thee O Thou Who penetratest all things, O All-Seeing God, O Lord of Utterance! Thou the Sufficing, Thou the Healing, Thou the Abiding, O Thou Abiding One!

I call on Thee O Manifest yet Hidden, O Unseen yet Renowned, O Onlooker sought by all! Thou the Sufficing, Thou the Healing, Thou the Abiding, O Thou Abiding One!

I call on Thee O Thou Who slayest the Lovers, O God of Grace to the wicked!

O Sufficer, I call on Thee, O Sufficer!

O Healer, I call on Thee, O Healer!

O Abider, I call on Thee, O Abider!

Thou the Ever-Abiding, O Thou Abiding One!

Sanctified art Thou, O my God! I beseech Thee by Thy generosity, whereby the portals of Thy bounty and grace were opened wide, whereby the Temple of Thy Holiness was established upon the throne of eternity; and by Thy mercy whereby Thou didst invite all created things unto the table of Thy bounties and bestowals; and by Thy grace whereby Thou didst respond, in Thine own Self with Thy word "Yea!" on behalf of all in heaven and earth, at the hour when Thy sovereignty and Thy grandeur stood revealed, at the dawn-time when the might of Thy dominion was made manifest. And again do I beseech Thee, by these most beauteous names, by these most noble and sublime attributes, and by Thy most Exalted Remembrance, and by Thy pure and spotless Beauty, and by Thy hidden Light in the most hidden pavilion, and by Thy Name, cloaked with the garment of affliction every morn and eve, to protect the bearer of this blessed Tablet, and whoso reciteth it, and whoso cometh upon it, and whoso passeth around the house wherein it is. Heal Thou, then, by it every sick, diseased and poor one, from every tribulation and distress, from every loathsome affliction and sorrow, and guide Thou by it whosoever desireth to enter upon the paths of Thy guidance, and the ways of Thy forgiveness and grace.

Thou art verily the Powerful, the All-Sufficing, the Healing, the Protector, the Giving, the Compassionate, the All-Generous, the All-Merciful.

—Bahá'u'lláh

ॐ ॐ ॐ

9

Resort ye, in times of sickness, to competent physicians; We have not set aside the use of material means, rather have We confirmed it through this Pen, which God hath made to be the Dawning-place of His shining and glorious Cause.

—Bahá'u'lláh

10

All true healing comes from God! There are two causes for sickness, one is material, the other spiritual. If the sickness is of the body, a material remedy is needed, if of the soul, a spiritual remedy.

If the heavenly benediction be upon us while we are being healed then only can we be made whole, for medicine is but the outward and visible means through which we obtain the heavenly healing. Unless the spirit be healed, the cure of the body is worth nothing. All is in the hands of God, and without Him there can be no health in us!

—'Abdu'l-Bahá

11

There are two ways of healing sickness, material means and spiritual means. The first is by the treatment of physicians; the second consisteth in prayers offered by the spiritual ones to God and in turning to Him. Both means should be used and practiced.

Illnesses which occur by reason of physical causes should be treated by doctors with medical remedies; those which are due to spiritual causes disappear through spiritual means. Thus an illness caused by affliction, fear, nervous impressions, will be healed more effectively by spiritual rather than by physical treatment. Hence, both kinds of treatment should be followed; they are not contradictory. Therefore thou shouldst also accept physical remedies inasmuch as these too have come from the mercy and favor of God, Who hath revealed and made manifest medical science so that His servants may profit from this kind of treatment also. Thou shouldst give equal attention to spiritual treatments, for they produce marvelous effects.

Now, if thou wishest to know the true remedy which will heal man from all sickness and will give him the health of the divine kingdom, know that it is the precepts and teachings of God. Focus thine attention upon them.

—*'Abdu'l-Bahá*

Times of Difficulty

1

O Thou Whose tests are a healing medicine to such as are nigh unto Thee, Whose sword is the ardent desire of all them that love Thee, Whose dart is the dearest wish of those hearts that yearn after Thee, Whose decree is the sole hope of them that have recognized Thy truth! I implore Thee, by Thy divine sweetness and by the splendors of the glory of Thy face, to send down upon us from Thy retreats on high that which will enable us to draw nigh unto Thee. Set, then, our feet firm, O my God, in Thy Cause, and enlighten our hearts with the effulgence of Thy knowledge, and illumine our breasts with the brightness of Thy names.

—Bahá'u'lláh

2

Glory to Thee, O my God! But for the tribulations which are sustained in Thy path, how could Thy true lovers be recognized; and were it not for the trials which are borne for love of Thee, how could the station of such as yearn for Thee be revealed? Thy might beareth me witness! The companions of all who adore Thee are the tears they shed, and the comforters of such as seek Thee are the groans they utter, and the food of them who haste to meet Thee is the fragments of their broken hearts.

How sweet to my taste is the bitterness of death suffered in Thy path, and how precious in my estimation are the shafts of Thine enemies when encountered for the sake of the exaltation of Thy word! Let me quaff in Thy Cause, O my God, whatsoever Thou didst desire, and send down upon me in Thy love all Thou didst ordain. By Thy glory! I wish only what Thou wishest, and cherish what Thou cherishest. In Thee have I, at all times, placed my whole trust and confidence.

Raise up, I implore Thee, O my God, as helpers to this Revelation such as shall be counted worthy of Thy name and of Thy sovereignty, that they may remember me among Thy creatures, and hoist the ensigns of Thy victory in Thy land.

Potent art Thou to do what pleaseth Thee. No God is there but Thee, the Help in Peril, the Self-Subsisting.

—Bahá'u'lláh

3

Glory be to Thee, O my God! I beg of Thee by Thy name, the Most Merciful, to protect Thy servants and Thy handmaidens when the tempests of trials pass over them, and Thy manifold tests assail them. Enable them, then, O my God, so to seek refuge within the stronghold of Thy love and of Thy Revelation, that neither Thine adversaries nor the wicked doers among Thy servants, who have broken Thy Covenant and Thy Testament, and turned away most disdainfully from the Dayspring of Thine Essence and the Revealer of Thy glory, may prevail against them.

They themselves, O my Lord, have waited at the door of Thy grace. Do Thou open it to their faces with the keys of Thy bountiful favors. Potent art Thou to do what Thou willest, and to ordain what Thou pleasest. These are the ones, O my Lord, who have set their faces towards Thee, and turned unto Thy habitation. Do with them, therefore, as becometh Thy mercy, which hath surpassed the worlds.

—*Bahá'u'lláh*

4

Glorified art Thou, O Lord my God! Every man of insight confesseth Thy sovereignty and Thy dominion, and every discerning eye perceiveth the greatness of Thy majesty and the compelling power of Thy might. The winds of tests are powerless to hold back them that enjoy near access to Thee from setting their faces towards the horizon of Thy glory, and the tempests of trials must fail to draw away and hinder such as are wholly devoted to Thy will from approaching Thy court.

Methinks, the lamp of Thy love is burning in their hearts, and the light of Thy tenderness is lit within their breasts. Adversities are incapable of estranging them from Thy Cause, and the vicissitudes of fortune can never cause them to stray from Thy pleasure.

I beseech Thee, O my God, by them and by the sighs which their hearts utter in their separation from Thee, to keep them safe from the mischief of Thine adversaries, and to nourish their souls with what Thou hast ordained for Thy loved ones on whom shall come no fear and who shall not be put to grief.

—*Bahá'u'lláh*

5

Lauded be Thy name, O my God! Thou beholdest how the tempestuous winds of tests have caused the steadfast in faith to tremble, and how the breath of trials hath stirred up those whose hearts had been firmly established, except such as have partaken of the Wine that is life indeed from the hands of the Manifestation of Thy name, the Most Merciful. These are the ones whom no word except Thy most exalted word can move, whom nothing whatever save the sweet smelling fragrance of the robe of Thy remembrance can enrapture, O Thou Who art the Possessor of all names and the Maker of earth and heaven!

I implore Thee, O Thou Who art the beloved Companion of Bahá, by Thy name, the All-Glorious, to keep safe these Thy servants under the shadow of the wings of Thine all-encompassing mercy, that the darts of the evil suggestions of the wicked doers among Thy creatures, who have disbelieved in Thy signs, may be kept back from them. No one on earth, O my Lord, can withstand Thy power, and none in all the kingdom of Thy names is able to frustrate Thy purpose. Show forth, then, the power of Thy sovereignty and of Thy dominion, and teach Thy loved ones what beseemeth them in Thy days.

Thou art, verily, the Almighty, the Most Exalted, the All-Glorious, the Most Great.

—*Bahá'u'lláh*

6

Dispel my grief by Thy bounty and Thy generosity, O God, my God, and banish mine anguish through Thy sovereignty and Thy might. Thou seest me, O my God, with my face set towards Thee at a time when sorrows have compassed me on every side. I implore Thee, O Thou Who art the Lord of all being, and overshadowest all things visible and invisible, by Thy Name whereby Thou hast subdued the hearts and the souls of men, and by the billows of the Ocean of Thy mercy and the splendors of the Daystar of Thy bounty, to number me with them whom nothing whatsoever hath deterred from setting their faces toward Thee, O Thou Lord of all names and Maker of the heavens!

Thou beholdest, O my Lord, the things which have befallen me in Thy days. I entreat Thee, by Him Who is the Dayspring of Thy names and the Dawning-Place of Thine attributes, to ordain for me what will enable me to arise to serve Thee and to extol Thy virtues. Thou art, verily, the Almighty, the Most Powerful, Who art wont to answer the prayers of all men!

And, finally, I beg of Thee by the light of Thy countenance to bless my affairs, and redeem my debts, and satisfy my needs. Thou art He to Whose power and to Whose dominion every tongue hath testified, and Whose majesty and Whose sovereignty every understanding heart hath acknowledged. No God is there but Thee, Who hearest and art ready to answer.

—*Bahá'u'lláh*

7

Is there any Remover of difficulties save God?
Say: Praised be God! He is God! All are His servants, and all abide by His bidding!

—The Báb

8

Thou knowest full well, O my God, that tribulations have showered upon me from all directions and that no one can dispel or transmute them except Thee. I know of a certainty, by virtue of my love for Thee, that Thou wilt never cause tribulations to befall any soul unless Thou desirest to exalt his station in Thy celestial Paradise and to buttress his heart in this earthly life with the bulwark of Thine all-compelling power, that it may not become inclined toward the vanities of this world. Indeed Thou art well aware that under all conditions I would cherish the remembrance of Thee far more than the ownership of all that is in the heavens and on the earth.

Strengthen my heart, O my God, in Thine obedience and in Thy love, and grant that I may be clear of the entire company of Thine adversaries. Verily, I swear by Thy glory that I yearn for naught besides Thyself, nor do I desire anything except Thy mercy, nor am I apprehensive of aught save

Thy justice. I beg Thee to forgive me as well as those whom Thou lovest, howsoever Thou pleasest. Verily, Thou art the Almighty, the Bountiful.

Immensely exalted art Thou, O Lord of the heavens and earth, above the praise of all men, and may peace be upon Thy faithful servants and glory be unto God, the Lord of all the worlds.

—The Báb

9

I adjure Thee by Thy might, O my God! Let no harm beset me in times of tests, and in moments of heedlessness guide my steps aright through Thine inspiration. Thou art God, potent art Thou to do what Thou desirest. No one can withstand Thy Will or thwart Thy Purpose.

—The Báb

ॐ   ॐ   ॐ

10

To the loyal soul, a test is but God's grace and favor; for the valiant doth joyously press forward to furious battle on the field of anguish, when the coward, whimpering with fright, will tremble and shake. So too, the proficient student, who hath with great competence mastered his subjects and committed them to memory, will happily exhibit his skills before his examiners on the day of his tests. So too will solid gold wondrously gleam and shine out in the assayer's fire.

It is clear, then, that tests and trials are, for sanctified souls, but God's bounty and grace, while to the weak, they are a calamity, unexpected and sudden.

These tests . . . do but cleanse the spotting of self from off the mirror of the heart, till the Sun of Truth can cast its rays thereon . . .

—'Abdu'l-Bahá

For Women

11

Convey thou unto the handmaids of the Merciful the message that when a test turneth violent they must stand unmoved, and faithful to their love for Bahá.* In winter come the storms, and the great winds blow, but then will follow spring in all its beauty, adorning hill and plain with perfumed plants and red anemones, fair to see. Then will the birds trill out upon the branches their songs of joy, and sermonize in lilting tones from the pulpits of the trees. Erelong shall ye bear witness that the lights are

---

* Bahá'u'lláh.

streaming forth, the banners of the realm above are waving, the sweet scents of the All-Merciful are wafted abroad, the hosts of the Kingdom are marching down, the angels of heaven are rushing forward, and the Holy Spirit is breathing upon all those regions. On that day thou shalt behold the waverers, men and women alike, frustrated of their hopes and in manifest loss. This is decreed by the Lord, the Revealer of Verses.

As to thee, blessed art thou, for thou art steadfast in the Cause of God, firm in His Covenant.* I beg of Him to bestow upon thee a spiritual soul, and the life of the Kingdom, and to make thee a leaf verdant and flourishing on the Tree of Life, that thou mayest serve the handmaids of the Merciful with spirituality and good cheer.

Thy generous Lord will assist thee to labor in His vineyard and will cause thee to be the means of spreading the spirit of unity among His handmaids. He will make thine inner eye to see with the light of knowledge, He will forgive thy sins and transform them into goodly deeds. Verily He is the Forgiving, the Compassionate, the Lord of immeasurable grace.

—'Abdu'l-Bahá

---

* The binding agreement between God and humanity that God will provide guidance to humankind and that humankind will accept it.

12

O thou who hast bowed thyself down in prayer before the Kingdom of God! Blessed art thou, for the beauty of the divine Countenance hath enraptured thy heart, and the light of inner wisdom hath filled it full, and within it shineth the brightness of the Kingdom. Know thou that God is with thee under all conditions, and that He guardeth thee from the changes and chances of this world and hath made thee a handmaid in His mighty vineyard.

—'Abdu'l-Bahá

13

O thou handmaid aflame with the fire of God's love! Grieve thou not over the troubles and hardships of this nether world, nor be thou glad in times of ease and comfort, for both shall pass away. This present life is even as a swelling wave, or a mirage, or drifting shadows. Could ever a distorted image on the desert serve as refreshing waters? No, by the Lord of Lords! Never can reality and the mere semblance of reality be one, and wide is the difference between fancy and fact, between truth and the phantom thereof.

Know thou that the Kingdom is the real world, and this nether place is only its shadow stretching out. A shadow hath no life of its own;

its existence is only a fantasy, and nothing more; it is but images reflected in water, and seeming as pictures to the eye.

Rely upon God. Trust in Him. Praise Him, and call Him continually to mind. He verily turneth trouble into ease, and sorrow into solace, and toil into utter peace. He verily hath dominion over all things.

If thou wouldst hearken to my words, release thyself from the fetters of whatsoever cometh to pass. Nay rather, under all conditions thank thou thy loving Lord, and yield up thine affairs unto His Will that worketh as He pleaseth. This verily is better for thee than all else, in either world.

—*'Abdu'l-Bahá*

Assistance

1

I implore Thee to assist me and them that love me to magnify Thy Word, and to endow us with such strength that the ills of this world and its tribulations will be powerless to hinder us from remembering Thee and from extolling Thy virtues. Powerful art Thou to do all things; resplendent art Thou above all things.

—*Bahá'u'lláh*

2

O Thou Whose face is the object of my adoration, Whose beauty is my sanctuary, Whose habitation is my goal, Whose praise is my hope, Whose providence is my companion, Whose love is the cause of my being, Whose mention is my solace, Whose nearness is my desire, Whose presence is my dearest wish and highest aspiration, I entreat Thee not to withhold from me the things Thou didst ordain for the chosen ones among Thy servants. Supply me, then, with the good of this world and of the next.

Thou, truly, art the King of all men. There is no God but Thee, the Ever-Forgiving, the Most Generous.

—*Bahá'u'lláh*

3

Lord! Pitiful are we, grant us Thy favor; poor, bestow upon us a share from the ocean of Thy wealth; needy, do Thou satisfy us; abased, give us Thy glory. The fowls of the air and the beasts of the field receive their meat each day from Thee, and all beings partake of Thy care and loving-kindness.

Deprive not this feeble one of Thy wondrous grace and vouchsafe by Thy might unto this helpless soul Thy bounty.

Give us our daily bread, and grant Thine increase in the necessities of life, that we may be dependent on none other but Thee, may commune wholly with Thee, may walk in Thy ways and declare Thy mysteries. Thou art the Almighty and the Loving and the Provider of all mankind.

—'Abdu'l-Bahá

4

O Thou kind Lord! We are servants of Thy Threshold, taking shelter at Thy holy Door. We seek no refuge save only this strong pillar, turn nowhere for a haven but unto Thy safe-keeping. Protect us, bless us, support us, make us such that we shall love but Thy good pleasure, utter only Thy praise, follow only the pathway of truth, that we may become rich enough to dispense with all save Thee, and receive our gifts from the sea of Thy beneficence, that we may ever strive to exalt Thy Cause and to spread Thy sweet savors far and wide, that we may become oblivious of self and occupied only with Thee, and disown all else and be caught up in Thee.

O Thou Provider, O Thou Forgiver! Grant us Thy grace and loving-kindness, Thy gifts and Thy bestowals, and sustain us, that we may attain our goal. Thou art the Powerful, the Able, the Knower, the Seer; and, verily, Thou art the Generous, and, verily, Thou art the All-Merciful, and, verily, Thou art the Ever-Forgiving, He to Whom repentance is due, He Who forgiveth even the most grievous of sins.

—'Abdu'l-Bahá

5

Remove not, O Lord, the festal board that hath been spread in Thy Name, and extinguish not the burning flame that hath been kindled by Thine unquenchable fire. Withhold not from flowing that living water of Thine that murmureth with the melody of Thy glory and Thy remembrance, and deprive not Thy servants from the fragrance of Thy sweet savors breathing forth the perfume of Thy love.

Lord! Turn the distressing cares of Thy holy ones into ease, their hardship into comfort, their abasement into glory, their sorrow into blissful joy, O Thou that holdest in Thy grasp the reins of all mankind!

Thou art, verily, the One, the Single, the Mighty, the All-Knowing, the All-Wise.

—'Abdu'l-Bahá

For Women

6

Magnified be Thy name, O Thou in Whose grasp are the reins of the souls of all them that have recognized Thee, and in Whose right hand are the destinies of all that are in heaven and all that are on earth! Thou doest, through the power of Thy might, what Thou willest, and ordainest, by an act of Thy volition, what Thou pleasest. The will of the most resolute of men is as nothing when compared with the compelling evidences of Thy will, and the determination of the most inflexible among Thy creatures is dissipated before the manifold revelations of Thy purpose.

Thou art He Who, through a word of Thy mouth, hath so enravished the hearts of Thy chosen ones that they have, in their love for Thee, detached themselves from all except Thyself, and laid down their lives and sacrificed their souls in Thy path, and borne, for Thy sake, what none of Thy creatures hath borne.

I am one of Thy handmaidens, O my Lord! I have turned my face towards the habitation of Thy mercy, and have sought the wonders of Thy manifold favors, inasmuch as all the members of my body proclaim Thee to be the All-Bounteous, He Whose grace is immense.

O Thou Whose face is the object of my adoration, Whose beauty is my sanctuary, Whose court is my goal, Whose remembrance is my wish, Whose affection is my solace, Whose love is my begetter, Whose praise is my companion, Whose nearness is my hope, Whose presence is my greatest longing and supreme aspiration! Disappoint me not, I entreat Thee, by withholding from me the things Thou didst ordain for the chosen ones among Thy handmaidens, and supply me with the good of this world and of the world to come.

Thou art, verily, the Lord of creation. No God is there beside Thee, the Ever-Forgiving, the Most Bountiful.

—*Bahá'u'lláh*

঵   ঵   ঵

7

Today, humanity is bowed down with trouble, sorrow and grief, no one escapes; the world is wet with tears; but, thank God, the remedy is at our doors. Let us turn our hearts away from the world of matter and live in the spiritual world! It alone can give us freedom! If we are hemmed in by difficulties we have only to call upon God, and by His great Mercy we shall be helped.

If sorrow and adversity visit us, let us turn our faces to the Kingdom and heavenly consolation will be outpoured.

If we are sick and in distress let us implore God's healing, and He will answer our prayer.

When our thoughts are filled with the bitterness of this world, let us turn our eyes to the sweetness of God's compassion and He will send us heavenly calm! If we are imprisoned in the material world, our spirit can soar into the Heavens and we shall be free indeed!

When our days are drawing to a close let us think of the eternal worlds, and we shall be full of joy!

—'Abdu'l-Bahá

8

Remember not your own limitations; the help of God will come to you. Forget yourself. God's help will surely come!

When you call on the Mercy of God waiting to reinforce you, your strength will be tenfold.

—'Abdu'l-Bahá

.

Protection

1

Praised be Thou, O Lord my God! This is Thy servant who hath quaffed from the hands of Thy grace the wine of Thy tender mercy, and tasted of the savor of Thy love in Thy days. I beseech Thee, by the embodiments of Thy names whom no grief can hinder from rejoicing in Thy love or from gazing on Thy face, and whom all the hosts of the heedless are powerless to cause to turn aside from the path of Thy pleasure, to supply him with the good things Thou dost possess, and to raise him up to such heights that he will regard the world even as a shadow that vanisheth swifter than the twinkling of an eye.

Keep him safe also, O my God, by the power of Thine immeasurable majesty, from all that Thou abhorrest. Thou art, verily, his Lord and the Lord of all worlds.

—*Bahá'u'lláh*

2

O God, my God! I have set out from my home, holding fast unto the cord of Thy love, and I have committed myself wholly to Thy care and Thy protection. I entreat Thee by Thy power through which Thou didst protect Thy loved ones from the wayward and the perverse, and from every contumacious oppressor, and every wicked doer who hath strayed far from Thee, to keep me safe by Thy bounty and Thy grace. Enable me, then, to return to my home by Thy power and Thy might. Thou art, truly, the Almighty, the Help in Peril, the Self-Subsisting.

—*Bahá'u'lláh*

3

O my God, my Master, the Goal of my desire! This, Thy servant, seeketh to sleep in the shelter of Thy mercy, and to repose beneath the canopy of Thy grace, imploring Thy care and Thy protection.

I beg of Thee, O my Lord, by Thine eye that sleepeth not, to guard mine eyes from beholding aught beside Thee. Strengthen, then, their vision that they may discern Thy signs, and behold the Horizon of Thy Revelation. Thou art He before the revelations of Whose omnipotence the quintessence of power hath trembled.

No God is there but Thee, the Almighty, the All-Subduing, the Unconditioned.

—*Bahá'u'lláh*

4

Glory be to Thee, O God! Thou art the God Who hath existed before all things, Who will exist after all things and will last beyond all things. Thou art the God Who knoweth all things, and is supreme over all things. Thou art the God Who dealeth mercifully with all things, Who judgeth between all things and Whose vision embraceth all things. Thou art God my Lord, Thou art aware of my position, Thou dost witness my inner and outer being.

Grant Thy forgiveness unto me and unto the believers who responded to Thy Call. Be Thou my sufficing helper against the mischief of whosoever may desire to inflict sorrow upon me or wish me ill. Verily, Thou art the Lord of all created things. Thou dost suffice everyone, while no one can be self-sufficient without Thee.

—The Báb

5

In the Name of God, the Lord of overpowering majesty, the All-Compelling.

Hallowed be the Lord in Whose hand is the source of dominion. He createth whatsoever He willeth by His Word of command "Be," and it is. His hath been the power of authority heretofore, and it shall remain His hereafter. He maketh victorious whomsoever He pleaseth, through the potency of His behest. He is in truth the Powerful, the Almighty. Unto Him pertaineth all glory and majesty in the kingdoms of Revelation and Creation and whatever lieth between them. Verily, He is the Potent, the All-Glorious. From everlasting He hath been the Source of indomitable strength and shall remain so unto everlasting. He is indeed the Lord of might and power. All the kingdoms of heaven and earth and whatever is between them are God's, and His power is supreme over all things. All the treasures of earth and heaven and everything between them are His, and His protection extendeth over all things. He is the Creator of the heavens and the earth and whatever lieth between them, and He truly is a witness over all things. He is the Lord of Reckoning for all that dwell in the heavens and on earth and whatever lieth between them, and truly God is swift to reckon. He setteth the measure assigned to all who are in the heavens and the earth and whatever is between them. Verily, He is the Supreme Protector. He holdeth in His grasp the keys of heaven and earth and of everything between them. At His Own pleasure doth He bestow gifts, through the power of His command. Indeed His grace encompasseth all, and He is the All-Knowing.

Say: God sufficeth unto me; He is the One Who holdeth in His grasp the kingdom of all things. Through the power of His hosts of heaven and earth and whatever lieth between them, He protecteth whomsoever among His servants He willeth. God, in truth, keepeth watch over all things.

Immeasurably exalted art Thou, O Lord! Protect us from what lieth in front of us and behind us, above our heads, on our right, on our left, below our feet and every other side to which we are exposed. Verily, Thy protection over all things is unfailing.

—*The Báb*

6

O God, my God! Shield Thy trusted servants from the evils of self and passion, protect them with the watchful eye of Thy loving-kindness from all rancor, hate and envy, shelter them in the impregnable stronghold of Thy care and, safe from the darts of doubtfulness, make them the manifestations of Thy glorious signs, illumine their faces with the effulgent rays shed from the Dayspring of Thy divine unity, gladden their hearts with the verses revealed from Thy holy kingdom, strengthen their loins by Thine all-swaying power that cometh from Thy realm of glory. Thou art the All-Bountiful, the Protector, the Almighty, the Gracious.

—'Abdu'l-Bahá

7

O my Lord! Thou knowest that the people are encircled with pain and calamities and are environed with hardships and trouble. Every trial doth attack man and every dire adversity doth assail him like unto the assault of a serpent. There is no shelter and asylum for him except under the wing of Thy protection, preservation, guard and custody.

O Thou the Merciful One! O my Lord! Make Thy protection my armor, Thy preservation my shield, humbleness before the door of Thy oneness my guard, and Thy custody and defense my fortress and my abode. Preserve me from the suggestions of self and desire, and guard me from every sickness, trial, difficulty and ordeal.

Verily, Thou art the Protector, the Guardian, the Preserver, the Sufficer, and verily, Thou art the Merciful of the Most Merciful.

—'Abdu'l-Bahá

8

O holy Lord! O Lord of loving-kindness! We stray about Thy dwelling, longing to behold Thy beauty, and loving all Thy ways. We are hapless, lowly, and of small account. We are paupers: show us mercy, give us bounty; look not upon our failings, hide Thou our endless sins. Whatever we are, still are we Thine, and what we speak and hear is praise of Thee, and it is Thy face we seek, Thy path we follow. Thou art the Lord of loving-kindness, we are sinners and astray and far from home. Wherefore, O Cloud of Mercy, grant us some drops of rain. O Flowering Bed of grace, send forth a fragrant breeze. O Sea of all bestowals, roll towards us a great wave. O Sun of Bounty, send down a shaft of light. Grant us pity, grant us grace. By Thy beauty, we come with no provision but our sins, with no good deeds to tell of, only hopes. Unless Thy concealing veil doth cover us, and Thy protection shield and cradle us, what power have these helpless souls to rise and serve Thee, what substance have these wretched ones to make a brave display? Thou Who art the Mighty, the All-Powerful, help us, favor us; withered as we are, revive us with showers from Thy clouds of grace; lowly as we are, illumine us with bright rays from the Day-Star of Thy oneness. Cast Thou these thirsty fish into the ocean of Thy mercy, guide Thou this lost caravan to the shelter of Thy singleness; to the wellspring of guidance lead Thou the ones who have wandered far astray, and grant to those who have missed the path a haven within the precincts of Thy might. Lift Thou to these parched lips the bounteous and soft-flowing waters of heaven, raise up these dead to everlasting life. Grant Thou to the blind eyes that will see. Make Thou the deaf to hear, the dumb to speak. Set Thou the dispirited ablaze, make Thou the heedless mindful, warn Thou the proud, awaken those who sleep.

Thou art the Mighty, Thou art the Bestower, Thou art the Loving. Verily Thou art the Beneficent, the Most Exalted.

—'Abdu'l-Bahá

❧ ❧ ❧

9

All the treasures of earth and heaven and everything between them are His, and His protection extendeth over all things. He is the Creator of the heavens and the earth and whatever lieth between them and He truly is a witness over all things.

—The Báb

10

The Old Testament says that God created man like unto His own image; in the Qur'án it says: "There is no difference in the Creation of God!" Think well, God has created all, cares for all, and all are under His protection. The policy of God is better than our policy. We are not as wise as God!

—'Abdu'l-Bahá

11

Discord deprives humanity of the eternal favors of God; therefore, we must forget all imaginary causes of difference and seek the very fundamentals of the divine religions in order that we may associate in perfect love and accord and consider humankind as one family, the surface of the earth as one nationality and all races as one humanity. Let us live under the protection of God, attaining eternal happiness in this world and everlasting life in the world to come.

—'Abdu'l-Bahá

12

We must strive in order that the power of the Holy Spirit may become effective throughout the world of mankind, that it may confer a new quickening life upon the body politic of the nations and peoples and that all may be guided to the protection and shelter of the Word of God. Then this human world will become angelic, earthly darkness pass away and celestial illumination flood the horizons, human defects be effaced and divine virtues become resplendent. This is possible and real, but only through the power of the Holy Spirit. Today the greatest need of the world is the animating, unifying presence of the Holy Spirit. Until it becomes effective, penetrating and interpenetrating hearts and spirits, and until perfect, reasoning faith shall be implanted in the minds of men, it will be impossible for the social body to be inspired with security and confidence.

—'Abdu'l-Bahá

Loss of a Loved One

1

Glory be to Thee, O Lord my God! Abase not him whom Thou hast exalted through the power of Thine everlasting sovereignty, and remove not far from Thee him whom Thou hast caused to enter the tabernacle of Thine eternity. Wilt Thou cast away, O my God, him whom thou hast overshadowed with Thy Lordship, and wilt Thou turn away from Thee, O my Desire, him to whom Thou hast been a refuge? Canst Thou degrade him whom Thou hast uplifted, or forget him whom Thou didst enable to remember Thee?

Glorified, immensely glorified art Thou! Thou art He Who from everlasting hath been the King of the entire creation and its Prime Mover, and Thou wilt to everlasting remain the Lord of all created things and their Ordainer. Glorified art Thou, O my God! If Thou ceasest to be merciful unto Thy servants, who, then, will show mercy unto them; and if Thou refusest to succor thy loved ones, who is there that can succor them?

Glorified, immeasurably glorified art Thou! Thou art adored in Thy truth, and Thee do we all, verily, worship; and Thou art manifest in Thy justice, and to Thee do we all, verily, bear witness. Thou art, in truth, beloved in Thy grace. No God is there but Thee, the Help in Peril, the Self-Subsisting.

—Bahá'u'lláh

2

O my God! O Thou forgiver of sins, bestower of gifts, dispeller of afflictions!

Verily, I beseech Thee to forgive the sins of such as have abandoned the physical garment and have ascended to the spiritual world.

O my Lord! Purify them from trespasses, dispel their sorrows, and change their darkness into light. Cause them to enter the garden of happiness, cleanse them with the most pure water, and grant them to behold Thy splendors on the loftiest mount.

—'Abdu'l-Bahá

3

O my God! O my God! Verily, Thy servant, humble before the majesty of Thy divine supremacy, lowly at the door of Thy oneness, hath believed in Thee and in Thy verses, hath testified to Thy word, hath been enkindled with the fire of Thy love, hath been immersed in the depths of the ocean of Thy knowledge, hath been attracted by Thy breezes, hath relied upon

Thee, hath offered his supplications to Thee, and hath been assured of Thy pardon and forgiveness. He hath abandoned this mortal life and hath flown to the kingdom of immortality, yearning for the favor of meeting Thee.

O Lord, glorify his station, shelter him under the pavilion of Thy supreme mercy, cause him to enter Thy glorious paradise, and perpetuate his existence in Thine exalted rose garden, that he may plunge into the sea of light in the world of mysteries.

Verily, Thou art the Generous, the Powerful, the Forgiver and the Bestower.

—*'Abdu'l-Bahá*

Loss of a Female Loved One
4

O my God, O Forgiver of sins and Dispeller of afflictions! O Thou Who art the Pardoner, the Merciful! I raise my suppliant hands to Thee, tearfully beseeching the court of Thy divine Essence to forgive, through Thy grace and clemency, Thy handmaiden who hath ascended unto the seat of truth. Cause her, O Lord, to be overshadowed by the clouds of Thy bounty and favor, immerse her in the ocean of Thy forgiveness and pardon, and enable her to enter that sanctified abode, Thy heavenly Paradise.

Thou art, verily, the Mighty, the Compassionate, the Generous, the Merciful.

—*'Abdu'l-Bahá*

5

O Lord, O Thou Whose mercy hath encompassed all, Whose forgiveness is transcendent, Whose bounty is sublime, Whose pardon and generosity are all-embracing, and the lights of Whose forgiveness are diffused throughout the world! O Lord of glory! I entreat Thee, fervently and tearfully, to cast upon Thy handmaiden who hath ascended unto Thee the glances of the eye of Thy mercy. Robe her in the mantle of Thy grace, bright with the ornaments of the celestial Paradise, and, sheltering her beneath the tree of Thy oneness, illumine her face with the lights of Thy mercy and compassion.

Bestow upon Thy heavenly handmaiden, O God, the holy fragrances born of the spirit of Thy forgiveness. Cause her to dwell in a blissful abode, heal her griefs with the balm of Thy reunion, and, in accordance with Thy will, grant her admission to Thy holy Paradise. Let the angels of Thy loving-kindness descend successively upon her, and shelter her beneath Thy blessed Tree. Thou art, verily, the Ever-Forgiving, the Most Generous, the All-Bountiful.

—*'Abdu'l-Bahá*

6

O Thou Kind Lord! This dearly cherished maidservant was attracted to Thee, and through reflection and discernment longed to attain Thy presence and enter Thy realms. With tearful eyes she fixed her gaze on the Kingdom of Mysteries. Many a night she spent in deep communion with Thee, and many a day she lived in intimate remembrance of Thee. At every morn she was mindful of Thee, and at every eve she centered her thoughts upon Thee. Like unto a singing nightingale she chanted Thy sacred verses, and like unto a mirror she sought to reflect Thy light.

O Thou Forgiver of sins! Open Thou the way for this awakened soul to enter Thy Kingdom, and enable this bird, trained by Thy hand, to soar in the eternal rose garden. She is afire with longing to draw nigh unto Thee; enable her to attain Thy presence. She is distraught and distressed in separation from Thee; cause her to be admitted into Thy Heavenly Mansion.

O Lord! We are sinners, but Thou art the Forgiver. We are submerged in the ocean of shortcomings, but Thou art the Pardoner, the Kind. Forgive our sins and bless us with Thine abundant grace. Grant us the privilege of beholding Thy Countenance, and give us the chalice of joy and bliss. We are captives of our own transgressions, and Thou art the King of bountiful favors. We are drowned in a sea of iniquities, and Thou art the Lord of infinite mercy. Thou art the Giver, the Glorious, the Eternal, the Bounteous; and Thou art the All-Gracious, the All-Merciful, the Omnipotent, He Who is the Bestower of gifts and the Forgiver of sins. Verily, Thou art He to Whom we turn for the remission of our failings, He Who is the Lord of lords.

—*'Abdu'l-Bahá*

❧   ❧   ❧

7

And now concerning thy question regarding the soul of man and its survival after death. Know thou of a truth that the soul, after its separation from the body, will continue to progress until it attaineth the presence of God, in a state and condition which neither the revolution of ages and centuries, nor the changes and chances of this world, can alter. It will endure as long as the Kingdom of God, His sovereignty, His dominion and power will endure. It will manifest the signs of God and His attributes, and will reveal His loving kindness and bounty. The movement of My Pen is stilled when it attempteth to befittingly describe the loftiness and glory

of so exalted a station. The honor with which
the Hand of Mercy will invest the soul is such
as no tongue can adequately reveal, nor any
other earthly agency describe. Blessed is the soul
which, at the hour of its separation from the
body, is sanctified from the vain imaginings of
the peoples of the world. Such a soul liveth and
moveth in accordance with the Will of its Creator, and entereth the all-highest Paradise.

—*Bahá'u'lláh*

8

Know thou that the soul of man is exalted
above, and is independent of all infirmities
of body or mind. That a sick person showeth
signs of weakness is due to the hindrances that
interpose themselves between his soul and his
body, for the soul itself remaineth unaffected by
any bodily ailments. Consider the light of the
lamp. Though an external object may interfere
with its radiance, the light itself continueth to
shine with undiminished power. In like manner,
every malady afflicting the body of man is an
impediment that preventeth the soul from man-
ifesting its inherent might and power. When it
leaveth the body, however, it will evince such ascendancy, and reveal such influence as no force
on earth can equal. Every pure, every refined

and sanctified soul will be endowed with tre-
mendous power, and shall rejoice with exceed-
ing gladness.

—*Bahá'u'lláh*

Loss of a Husband

9

O thou assured soul, thou maidservant of
God . . . ! Be not grieved at the death of
thy respected husband. He hath, verily, attained
the meeting of his Lord at the seat of Truth in
the presence of the potent King. Do not sup-
pose that thou hast lost him. The veil shall be
lifted and thou shalt behold his face illumined
in the Supreme Concourse. Just as God, the Exalted, hath said, "Him will We surely quicken
to a happy life." Supreme importance should be
attached, therefore, not to this first creation but
rather to the future life.

—*'Abdu'l-Bahá*

Loss of a Son

10

O thou beloved maidservant of God, although
the loss of a son is indeed heartbreaking
and beyond the limits of human endurance, yet
one who knoweth and understandeth is assured

that the son hath not been lost but, rather, hath stepped from this world into another, and she will find him in the divine realm. That reunion shall be for eternity, while in this world separation is inevitable and bringeth with it a burning grief.

Praise be unto God that thou hast faith, art turning thy face toward the everlasting Kingdom and believest in the existence of a heavenly world. Therefore be thou not disconsolate, do not languish, do not sigh, neither wail nor weep; for agitation and mourning deeply affect his soul in the divine realm.

That beloved child addresseth thee from the hidden world: "O thou kind Mother, thank divine Providence that I have been freed from a small and gloomy cage and, like the birds of the meadows, have soared to the divine world—a world which is spacious, illumined, and ever gay and jubilant. Therefore, lament not, O Mother, and be not grieved; I am not of the lost, nor have I been obliterated and destroyed. I have shaken off the mortal form and have raised my banner in this spiritual world. Following this separation is everlasting companionship. Thou shalt find me in the heaven of the Lord, immersed in an ocean of light."

—'Abdu'l-Bahá

Peace

1

O Thou Who art the Lord of Lords! I testify that Thou art the Lord of all creation, and the Educator of all beings, visible and invisible. I bear witness that Thy power hath encompassed the entire universe, and that the hosts of the earth can never dismay Thee, nor can the dominion of all peoples and nations deter Thee from executing Thy purpose. I confess that Thou hast no desire except the regeneration of the whole world, and the establishment of the unity of its peoples, and the salvation of all them that dwell therein.

—Bahá'u'lláh

2

O Thou compassionate Lord, Thou Who art generous and able! We are servants of Thine sheltered beneath Thy providence. Cast Thy glance of favor upon us. Give light to our eyes, hearing to our ears, and understanding and love to our hearts. Render our souls joyous and happy through Thy glad tidings. O Lord! Point out to us the pathway of Thy kingdom and resuscitate all of us through the breaths of the Holy Spirit. Bestow upon us life everlasting and confer upon us never-ending honor. Unify mankind and illumine the world of humanity. May we all follow Thy pathway, long for Thy good pleasure and seek the mysteries of Thy kingdom. O God! Unite us and connect our hearts with Thy indissoluble bond. Verily, Thou art the Giver, Thou art the Kind One and Thou art the Almighty.

—'Abdu'l-Bahá

3

O Thou kind Lord! O Thou Who art generous and merciful! We are the servants of Thy threshold and are gathered beneath the sheltering shadow of Thy divine unity. The sun of Thy mercy is shining upon all, and the clouds of Thy bounty shower upon all. Thy gifts encompass all, Thy loving providence sustains all, Thy protection overshadows all, and the glances of Thy favor are cast upon all. O Lord! Grant Thine infinite bestowals, and let the light of Thy guidance shine. Illumine the eyes, gladden the hearts with abiding joy. Confer a new spirit upon all people and bestow upon them eternal life. Unlock the gates of true understanding and let the light of faith shine resplendent. Gather all people beneath the shadow of Thy bounty and cause them to unite in harmony, so that they may become as the rays of one sun, as the waves of one ocean, and as the fruit of one tree. May they drink from the same fountain. May they be refreshed by the same breeze. May they receive illumination from the same source of light. Thou art the Giver, the Merciful, the Omnipotent.

—'Abdu'l-Bahá

4

O Divine Providence! This assemblage is composed of Thy friends who are attracted to Thy beauty and are set ablaze by the fire of Thy love. Turn these souls into heavenly angels, resuscitate them through the breath of Thy Holy Spirit, grant them eloquent tongues and resolute hearts, bestow upon them heavenly power and merciful susceptibilities, cause them to become the promulgators of the oneness of mankind and the cause of love and concord in the world of humanity, so that the perilous darkness of ignorant prejudice may vanish through the light of the Sun of Truth, this dreary world may become illumined, this material realm may absorb the rays of the world of spirit, these different colors may merge into one color and the melody of praise may rise to the kingdom of Thy sanctity.

Verily, Thou art the Omnipotent and the Almighty!

—'Abdu'l-Bahá

5

O Thou kind God! In the utmost state of humility and submission do we entreat and supplicate at Thy threshold, seeking Thine endless confirmations and illimitable assistance. O Thou Lord! Regenerate these souls, and confer upon them a new life. Animate the spirits, inform the hearts, open the eyes, and make the ears attentive. From Thine ancient treasury confer a new being and animus, and from Thy preexistent abode assist them to attain to new confirmations.

O God! Verily, the world is in need of reformation. Bestow upon it a new existence. Give it newness of thoughts, and reveal unto it heavenly sciences. Breathe into it a fresh spirit, and grant unto it a holier and higher purpose.

O God! Verily, Thou hast made this century radiant, and in it Thou hast manifested Thy merciful effulgence. Thou hast effaced the darkness of superstitions and permitted the light of assurance to shine. O God! Grant that these servants may be acceptable at Thy threshold. Reveal a new heaven, and spread out a new earth for habitation. Let a new Jerusalem descend from on high.

Bestow new thoughts, new life upon mankind. Endow souls with new perceptions, and confer upon them new virtues. Verily, Thou art the Almighty, the Powerful. Thou art the Giver, the Generous.

—'Abdu'l-Bahá

6

O Lord! Verily, the people are veiled and in a state of contention with each other, shedding the blood and destroying the possessions of each other. Throughout the world there is war and conflict. In every direction there is strife, bloodshed and ferocity.

O Lord! Guide human souls in order that they may turn away from warfare and battle, that they may become loving and kind to each other, that they may enter into affiliation and serve the oneness and solidarity of humanity.

O Lord! The horizons of the world are darkened by this dissension. O God! Illumine them, and through the lights of Thy love let the hearts become radiant. Through the blessing of Thy bestowal resuscitate the spirits until every soul shall perceive and act in accordance with Thy teachings. Thou art the Almighty. Thou art the Omniscient. Thou art the Seer. O Lord, be compassionate to all.

—'Abdu'l-Bahá

7

Thou kind Lord! Thou hast created all humanity from the same stock. Thou hast decreed that all shall belong to the same household. In Thy Holy Presence they are all Thy servants, and all mankind are sheltered beneath Thy Tabernacle; all have gathered together at Thy Table of Bounty; all are illumined through the light of Thy Providence.

O God! Thou art kind to all, Thou hast provided for all, dost shelter all, conferrest life upon all. Thou hast endowed each and all with talents and faculties, and all are submerged in the Ocean of Thy Mercy.

O Thou kind Lord! Unite all. Let the religions agree and make the nations one, so that they may see each other as one family and the whole earth as one home. May they live together in perfect harmony.

O God! Raise aloft the banner of the oneness of mankind.

O God! Establish the Most Great Peace.

Cement Thou, O God, the hearts together.

O Thou kind Father, God! Gladden our hearts through the fragrance of Thy love. Brighten our eyes through the Light of Thy Guidance. Delight our ears with the melody of Thy Word, and shelter us all in the Stronghold of Thy Providence.

Thou art the Mighty and Powerful, Thou art the Forgiving and Thou art the One Who overlooketh the shortcomings of all mankind.

—'Abdu'l-Bahá

ৡ   ৡ   ৡ

8

Please God, the peoples of the world may be led, as the result of the high endeavors exerted by their rulers and the wise and learned amongst men, to recognize their best interests. How long will humanity persist in its waywardness? How long will injustice continue? How long is chaos and confusion to reign amongst men? How long will discord agitate the face of society? . . . The winds of despair are, alas, blowing from every direction, and the strife that divideth and afflicteth the human race is daily increasing. The signs of impending convulsions and chaos can now be discerned, inasmuch as the prevailing order appeareth to be lamentably defective. I beseech God, exalted be His glory, that He may graciously awaken the peoples of the earth, may grant that the end of their conduct may be profitable unto them, and aid them to accomplish that which beseemeth their station.

—Bahá'u'lláh

9

If any man were to meditate on that which the Scriptures, sent down from the heaven of God's holy Will, have revealed, he would readily recognize that their purpose is that all men shall be regarded as one soul, so that the seal bearing the words "The Kingdom shall be God's" may be stamped on every heart, and the light of Divine bounty, of grace, and mercy may envelop all mankind. The One true God, exalted be His glory, hath wished nothing for Himself. The allegiance of mankind profiteth Him not, neither doth its perversity harm Him. . . . If the learned and worldly wise men of this age were to allow mankind to inhale the fragrance of fellowship and love, every understanding heart would apprehend the meaning of true liberty, and discover the secret of undisturbed peace and absolute composure.

—Bahá'u'lláh

10

It is self-evident that humanity is at variance. Human tastes differ; thoughts, native lands, races and tongues are many. The need of a collective center by which these differences may be counterbalanced and the people of the world be unified is obvious. Consider how nothing but a spiritual power can bring about this unification, for material conditions and mental aspects are so widely different that agreement and unity are not possible through outer means. It is possible, however, for all to become unified through one spirit, just as all may receive light from one sun. Therefore, assisted by the collective and divine center which is the law of God and the reality of His Manifestation, we can overcome these conditions until they pass away entirely and the races advance.

—'Abdu'l-Bahá

11

Man's glory and greatness do not consist in his being avid for blood and sharp of claw, in tearing down cities and spreading havoc, in butchering armed forces and civilians. What would mean a bright future for him would be his reputation for justice, his kindness to the entire population whether high or low, his building up countries and cities, villages and districts, his making life easy, peaceful and happy for his fellow beings, his laying down fundamental principles for progress, his raising the standards and increasing the wealth of the entire population.

—'Abdu'l-Bahá

12

Today there is no greater glory for man than that of service in the cause of the Most Great Peace. Peace is light, whereas war is darkness. Peace is life; war is death. Peace is guidance; war is error. Peace is the foundation of God; war is a satanic institution. Peace is the illumination of the world of humanity; war is the destroyer of human foundations. When we consider outcomes in the world of existence, we find that peace and fellowship are factors of up-building and betterment, whereas war and strife are the causes of destruction and disintegration. All created things are expressions of the affinity and cohesion of elementary substances, and nonexistence is the absence of their attraction and agreement. Various elements unite harmoniously in composition, but when these elements become discordant, repelling each other, decomposition and nonexistence result. Everything partakes of this nature and is subject to this principle, for the creative foundation in all its degrees and kingdoms is an expression or outcome of love. Consider the restlessness and agitation of the human world today because of war. Peace is health and construction; war is disease and dissolution. When the banner of truth is raised, peace becomes the cause of the welfare and advancement of the human world.

In all cycles and ages war has been a factor of derangement and discomfort, whereas peace and brotherhood have brought security and consideration of human interests. This distinction is especially pronounced in the present world conditions, for warfare in former centuries had not attained the degree of savagery and destructiveness which now characterizes it. If two nations were at war in olden times, ten or twenty thousand would be sacrificed, but in this century the destruction of one hundred thousand lives in a day is quite possible. So perfected has the science of killing become and so efficient the means and instruments of its accomplishment that a whole nation can be obliterated in a short time. Therefore, comparison with the methods and results of ancient warfare is out of the question.

According to an intrinsic law all phenomena of being attain to a summit and degree of consummation, after which a new order and condition is established. As the instruments and science of war have reached the degree of thoroughness and proficiency, it is hoped that the transformation of the human world is at hand and that in the coming centuries all the energies and inventions of man will be utilized in promoting the interests of peace and brotherhood.

—*'Abdu'l-Bahá*

13

I charge you all that each one of you concentrate all the thoughts of your heart on love and unity. When a thought of war comes, oppose it by a stronger thought of peace. A thought of hatred must be destroyed by a more powerful thought of love. Thoughts of war bring destruction to all harmony, well-being, restfulness and content.

Thoughts of love are constructive of brotherhood, peace, friendship, and happiness.

When soldiers of the world draw their swords to kill, soldiers of God clasp each other's hands! So may all the savagery of man disappear by the Mercy of God, working through the pure in heart and the sincere of soul. Do not think the peace of the world an ideal impossible to attain!

Nothing is impossible to the Divine Benevolence of God.

If you desire with all your heart, friendship with every race on earth, your thought, spiritual and positive, will spread; it will become the desire of others, growing stronger and stronger, until it reaches the minds of all men.

—'Abdu'l-Bahá

References

CHILDREN

1. *Bahá'í Prayers,* pp. 32–33.
2. Ibid., p. 33.
3. Ibid., pp. 33–34.
4. Ibid., p. 28.
5. Ibid., p. 28.
6. Ibid., pp. 28–29.
7. Ibid., p. 33.
8. Ibid., pp. 30–31.
9. Ibid., p. 254.
10. *Selections from the Writings of 'Abdu'l-Bahá,* no. 106.1–2.
11. Ibid., no. 115.2–4.
12. Ibid., no. 95.2.

PARENTS

1. *Gleanings,* no. 138.4–5.
2. *Bahá'í Prayers,* p. 64.
3. *Family Life,* p. 33.
4. *Lights of Guidance,* no. 762.
5. *Kitáb-i-Aqdas,* pp. 136–37.
6. *Some Answered Questions,* pp. 231–32.
7. *Family Life,* pp. 36–37.

PARENTING

PRAYER FOR EXPECTANT MOTHERS

1. *Bahá'í Prayers*, pp. 249–50.

2. Kitáb-i-Aqdas, ¶48.

3. *Selections from the Writings of 'Abdu'l-Bahá*, no. 103.5.

4. Ibid., no. 102.3.

5. *The Compilation of Compilations*, 1:263.

MOTHERHOOD

6. *Selections from the Writings of 'Abdu'l-Bahá*, no. 95.2.

7. Ibid., no. 96.1–2.

8. Ibid., no. 113.1–3.

9. Ibid., no. 95.1.

10. Ibid., no. 114.1.

MARRIAGE

1. *Bahá'í Prayers*, pp. 118–19.

2. Ibid., p. 120.

3. Ibid., p. 121.

4. Kitáb-i-Aqdas, ¶63.

5. *Bahá'í Prayers*, pp. 117–18.

6. *Selections from the Writings of 'Abdu'l-Bahá*, no. 86.1.

7. Ibid., no. 84.2–4.

8. Ibid., no. 92.1–3.

9. *Family Life*, p. 5.

LOVE

1. *Prayers and Meditations,* pp. 37–39.

2. Ibid., pp. 56–57.

3. Ibid., p. 145.

4. *Gleanings,* no. 153.5.

5. *Selections from the Writings of 'Abdu'l-Bahá,* no. 12.1.

6. Ibid., no. 1.7.

7. Ibid., no. 174.2–4.

EQUALITY OF THE SEXES

1. *Bahá'í Prayers,* p. 56.

2. *Compilation of Compilations,* 2:2094.

3. Ibid., 2:2145.

4. *Selections from the Writings of 'Abdu'l-Bahá,* no. 227.18.

5. *Promulgation of Universal Peace,* pp. 102, 104–5.

6. Ibid., p. 106.

7. Ibid., pp. 184–85.

8. Ibid., p. 253.

9. *Paris Talks,* no. 40.33.

10. *Promulgation of Universal Peace,* pp. 242–43.

11. *Paris Talks,* no. 59.5.

UNITY

1. *Bahá'í Prayers,* p. 238.

2. *Promulgation of Universal Peace,* pp. 328–29.

3. *Gleanings,* no. 110.1.

4. Ibid., no. 112.1

5. *Tablets of Bahá'u'lláh,* p. 138.

6. *Selections from the Writings of 'Abdu'l-Bahá,* no. 68.2–3.

7. *Promulgation of Universal Peace,* pp. 456–57.

8. Ibid., p. 128.

9. *Selections from the Writings of 'Abdu'l-Bahá,* no. 1.2–4.

10. *Tablets of the Divine Plan,* p. 103.

11. *Selections from the Writings of 'Abdu'l-Bahá,* no. 221.6.

PRAISE AND THANKSGIVING

1. *Bahá'í Prayers,* pp. 19–20.

2. Ibid., p. 4.

3. Ibid., pp. 51–52.

4. Ibid., pp. 52–54.

5. Ibid., p. 60.

6. Ibid., pp. 135–36.

7. Ibid., pp. 136–38.

8. Ibid., pp. 138–39.

9. *Prayers and Meditations,* pp. 199–200.

10. *Bahá'í Prayers,* pp. 40–41.

11. Ibid., pp. 81.

12. Ibid., pp. 89–90.

13. *Selections from the Writings of 'Abdu'l-Bahá,* no. 2.1–5.

14. Ibid., no. 19.1–2.

15. *Bahá'í Prayers,* pp. 212–14.

16. *Promulgation of Universal Peace*, p. 359.
17. *'Abdu'l-Bahá in London*, p. 20.
18. *Compilation of Compilations*, 1:842.

GUIDANCE

1. *Bahá'í Prayers*, pp. 68–69.
2. Ibid., pp. 199–200.
3. Ibid., p. 230.
4. Ibid., p. 191.
5. Ibid., pp. 115–16.
6. Ibid., pp. 71.
7. Ibid., pp. 71–72.
8. Ibid., pp. 191–93.
9. Ibid., p. 29.
10. *Gleanings*, no. 81.1.
11. *Paris Talks*, no. 18.5–7.
12. *'Abdu'l-Bahá in London*, p. 38.
13. *Paris Talks*, no. 5.24.

SPIRITUAL GROWTH

1. *Prayers and Meditations*, p. 227.
2. *Bahá'í Prayers*, pp. 163–64.
3. Ibid., p. 167.
4. *Promulgation of Universal Peace*, p. 646.
5. *Bahá'í Prayers*, pp. 56–57.
6. Ibid., pp. 175–76.
7. Ibid., p. 201.
8. *Paris Talks*, no. 40.35.
9. Ibid., no. 14.10.

10. *Selections from the Writings of 'Abdu'l-Bahá,* no. 174.5.

11. *'Abdu'l-Bahá in London,* p. 107.

ACQUIRING VIRTUES

1. *Bahá'í Prayers,* pp. 164–65.
2. *Compilation of Compilations,* 2:2020.
3. *Bahá'í Prayers,* pp. 88–89.
4. Ibid., p. 29.
5. *Gleanings,* no. 109.2.
6. Ibid., no. 134.2.
7. *Tablets of Bahá'u'lláh,* p. 37.
8. *Gleanings,* no. 96.3.
9. *Paris Talks,* no. 18.2–3.
10. Ibid., no. 36.6–10.
11. *Promulgation of Universal Peace,* pp. 151–52.
12. Ibid., p. 636.
13. *Some Answered Questions,* pp. 235–36.
14. *Bahá'í World Faith,* p. 384.

LETTING GO OF WORLDLY MATTERS

1. *Tablets of Bahá'u'lláh,* p. 59.
2. *Prayers and Meditations,* pp. 25–26.
3. Ibid., pp. 59–60.
4. Ibid., pp. 206–7.
5. *Selections from the Writings of the Báb,* no. 7:17:1–2.
6. *Selections from the Writings of 'Abdu'l-Bahá,* no. 146.9–11.

7. *Bahá'í Prayers,* pp. 218–19.

8. *Seven Valleys,* pp. 21–22.

9. Kitáb-i-Íqán, ¶2.

10. Ibid., ¶213.

11. *Summons of the Lord of Hosts,* no. 1.83.

12. *Paris Talks,* no. 9.26.

Drawing Closer to God

1. *Bahá'í Prayers,* pp. 224–25.

2. Ibid., pp. 47–48.

3. Ibid., pp. 240–41.

4. Ibid., pp. 50–51.

5. Ibid., pp. 128–30.

6. Ibid., pp. 190–91.

7. *Selections from the Writings of the Báb,* no. 7:29:1–6.

8. *Selections from the Writings of 'Abdu'l-Bahá,* no. 19.15–18.

9. *Hidden Words,* Arabic, no. 6.

10. *Gleanings,* no. 14.18.

11. Ibid., no. 29.2.

12. *Promulgation of Universal Peace,* pp. 203–4.

Steadfastness

1. *Prayers and Meditations,* pp. 188–89.

2. Ibid., pp. 219–20.

3. *Bahá'í Prayers,* pp. 186–88.

4. *Prayers and Meditations,* pp. 222–23.

5. *Bahá'í Prayers,* pp. 20–22.

6. Ibid., pp. 69–70.

7. Ibid., pp. 176–77.

8. *Gleanings,* no. 134.3.

9. Ibid., no. 86.2.

10. *Tablets of Bahá'u'lláh,* p. 91.

11. *Selections from the Writings of 'Abdu'l-Bahá,* no. 2.15.

HEALING

1. *Bahá'í Prayers,* pp. 95–96.

2. Ibid., p. 96.

3. Ibid., pp. 96–97.

4. Ibid., pp. 97–99.

5. *Prayers and Meditations,* pp. 102–3.

FOR WOMEN

6. *Bahá'í Prayers,* pp. 99–100.

FOR INFANTS

7. Ibid., pp. 100–102.

THE LONG HEALING PRAYER

8. Ibid., pp. 102–10.

9. Kitáb-i-Aqdas, ¶113.

10. *Paris Talks,* no. 3.1–2.

11. *Selections from the Writings of 'Abdu'l-Bahá,* no. 133.1–3.

Times of Difficulty

1. *Bahá'í Prayers,* p. 220.
2. Ibid., pp. 220–22.
3. *Prayers and Meditations,* pp. 231–32.
4. Ibid., p. 3.
5. Ibid., pp. 15–16.
6. Ibid., pp. 247–48.
7. *Bahá'í Prayers,* p. 226.
8. Ibid., pp. 226–27.
9. Ibid., p. 227.
10. *Selections from the Writings of 'Abdu'l-Bahá,* no. 155.2–4.

For Women

11. Ibid., no. 141.4–6.
12. Ibid., no. 91.1.
13. Ibid., no. 150.1–4.

Assistance

1. *Prayers and Meditations,* p. 101.
2. *Bahá'í Prayers,* p. 19.
3. Ibid., pp. 22–23.
4. Ibid., pp. 23–24.
5. Ibid., pp. 24–25.

For Women

6. *Prayers and Meditations,* pp. 163–64.

7. *Paris Talks,* no. 35.7–11.

8. Ibid., no. 9.24–25.

PROTECTION

1. *Bahá'í Prayers,* pp. 145–46.

2. Ibid., p. 147.

3. *Prayers and Meditations,* p. 263

4. *Bahá'í Prayers,* pp. 150–51.

5. Ibid., pp. 151–53.

6. Ibid., pp. 153–54.

7. Ibid., p. 154.

8. *Selections from the Writings of 'Abdu'l-Bahá,* no. 2.10–11.

9. *Compilation of Compilations,* 2:1656.

10. *'Abdu'l-Bahá in London,* p. 55.

11. *Promulgation of Universal Peace,* p. 153.

12. Ibid., p. 457.

LOSS OF A LOVED ONE

1. *Bahá'í Prayers,* pp. 37–38.

2. Ibid., p. 41.

3. Ibid., pp. 41–42.

LOSS OF A FEMALE LOVED ONE

4. Ibid., pp. 43–44.

5. Ibid., pp. 44–45.

6. Ibid., pp. 45–46.

7. *Gleanings,* no. 81.1.

8. Ibid., no. 80.2.

Loss of a Husband

9. *Selections from the Writings of 'Abdu'l-Bahá,* no. 165.4.

Loss of a Son

10. Ibid., no. 171.1–3.

Peace

1. *Gleanings,* no. 115.7.

2. *Bahá'í Prayers,* p. 112.

3. *Promulgation of Universal Peace,* p. 160.

4. *Selections from the Writings of 'Abdu'l-Bahá,* no. 68.10–11.

5. *Promulgation of Universal Peace,* p. 385.

6. Ibid., p. 384.

7. *Bahá'í Prayers,* pp. 113–15.

8. *Gleanings,* no. 110.1.

9. Ibid., no. 122.1.

10. *Promulgation of Universal Peace,* p. 227.

11. *Secret of Divine Civilization,* p. 67.

12. *Promulgation of Universal Peace,* pp. 170–71.

13. *Paris Talks,* no. 6.7–11.

Bibliography

Works of Bahá'u'lláh

Gleanings from the Writings of Bahá'u'lláh. Translated by Shoghi Effendi. Wilmette, IL: Bahá'í Publishing, 2005.

The Hidden Words. Translated by Shoghi Effendi. Wilmette, IL: Bahá'í Publishing, 2002.

The Kitáb-i-Aqdas: The Most Holy Book. 1st pocket-size ed. Wilmette, IL: Bahá'í Publishing Trust, 1993.

The Kitáb-i-Íqán: The Book of Certitude. Translated by Shoghi Effendi. Wilmette, IL: Bahá'í Publishing, 2003.

Prayers and Meditations. Translated by Shoghi Effendi. 1st pocket-size ed. Wilmette, IL: Bahá'í Publishing Trust, 1987.

The Seven Valleys and The Four Valleys. New ed. Translated by Ali-Kuli Khan and Marzieh Gail. Wilmette, IL: Bahá'í Publishing Trust, 1991.

The Summons of the Lord of Hosts: Tablets of Bahá'u'lláh. Wilmette, IL: Bahá'í Publishing, 2006.

Tablets of Bahá'u'lláh revealed after the Kitáb-i-Aqdas. Compiled by the Research Department of the Universal House of Justice. Translated by Habib Taherzadeh et al. Wilmette, IL: Bahá'í Publishing Trust, 1988.

WORKS OF THE BÁB

Selections from the Writings of the Báb. Compiled by the Research Department of the Universal House of Justice. Translated by Habib Taherzadeh et al. Wilmette, IL: Bahá'í Publishing Trust, 2006.

WORKS OF 'ABDU'L-BAHÁ

'Abdu'l-Bahá in London: Addresses and Notes of Conversations. London: Bahá'í Publishing Trust, 1982.

Paris Talks: Addresses Given By 'Abdu'l-Bahá in Paris in 1911. Wilmette, IL: Bahá'í Publishing, 2006.

Promulgation of Universal Peace: Talks Delivered by 'Abdu'l-Bahá during His Visit to the United States and Canada in 1912. Compiled by Howard MacNutt. Wilmette, IL: Bahá'í Publishing, 2007.

Selections from the Writings of 'Abdu'l-Bahá. Compiled by the Research Department of the Universal House of Justice. Translated by a Committee at the Bahá'í World Center and Marzieh Gail. 1st pocket-size ed. Wilmette, IL: Bahá'í Publishing Trust, 1996.

Some Answered Questions. Compiled and translated by Laura Clifford Barney. 1st pocket-size ed. Wilmette, IL: Bahá'í Publishing Trust, 1984.

Tablets of the Divine Plan: Revealed by 'Abdu'l-Bahá to the North America Bahá'ís. 1st pocket-sized ed. Wilmette, IL: Bahá'í Publishing Trust, 1993.

COMPILATIONS OF BAHÁ'Í WRITINGS

Bahá'u'lláh and 'Abdu'l-Bahá. *Bahá'í World Faith: Selected Writings of Bahá'u'lláh and 'Abdu'l-Bahá.* 2nd ed. Wilmette, IL: Bahá'í Publishing Trust, 1976.

Bahá'u'lláh, the Báb, and 'Abdu'l-Bahá. *Bahá'í Prayers: A Selection of Prayers Revealed by Bahá'u'lláh, the Báb, and 'Abdu'l-Bahá.* New ed. Wilmette, IL: Bahá'í Publishing Trust, 2002.

Bahá'u'lláh, the Báb, 'Abdu'l-Bahá, Shoghi Effendi, and the Universal House of Justice. *The Compilation of Compilations,* 2 volumes. Australia: Bahá'í Publications Australia, 1991.

Bahá'u'lláh, the Báb, 'Abdu'l-Bahá, Shoghi Effendi, and the Universal House of Justice. *Family Life: A Compilation of Extracts from the Bahá'í Writings and from Letters Written on Behalf of Shoghi Effendi and the Universal House of Justice.* Wilmette, IL: Bahá'í Publishing Trust, 2008.

Helen Hornby, compiler. *Lights of Guidance: A Bahá'í Reference File.* New ed. New Delhi, India: Bahá'í Publishing Trust, 1994.

Alphabetical Index to First Lines of Prayers and Meditations

PUBLISHING
and the Bahá'í Faith

Bahá'í Publishing produces books based on the teachings of the Bahá'í Faith. Founded over 160 years ago, the Bahá'í Faith has spread to some 235 nations and territories and is now accepted by more than five million people. The word "Bahá'í" means "follower of Bahá'u'lláh." Bahá'u'lláh, the founder of the Bahá'í Faith, asserted that He is the Messenger of God for all of humanity in this day. The cornerstone of His teachings is the establishment of the spiritual unity of humankind, which will be achieved by personal transformation and the application of clearly identified spiritual principles. Bahá'ís also believe that there is but one religion and that all the Messengers of God—among them Abraham, Zoroaster, Moses, Krishna, Buddha, Jesus, and Muḥammad—have progressively revealed its nature. Together, the world's great religions are expressions of a single, unfolding divine plan. Human beings, not God's Messengers, are the source of religious divisions, prejudices, and hatreds.

The Bahá'í Faith is not a sect or denomination of another religion, nor is it a cult or a social movement. Rather, it is a globally recognized independent world religion founded on new books of scripture revealed by Bahá'u'lláh.

Bahá'í Publishing is an imprint of the National Spiritual Assembly of the Bahá'ís of the United States.

For more information about the Bahá'í Faith,
or to contact Bahá'ís near you, visit
http://www.bahai.us/
or call
1-800-22-unite

disorder, and dementia can influence a person's creative impulse and how the interplay of creativity and spirituality can help a person deal with trauma and hardship.

Drawing on principles found in the teachings of the Bahá'í Faith, Dr. Ghadirian considers the meaning of suffering, its place in human society, and how it can lead to a closer, happier relationship with God, as well as a better relationship with oneself and with others. Indeed, many of those who have suffered the most in life have found new meaning through adversity and have emerged victorious. Their encounters with adversity and their victory over it suggest the presence of another force beyond understanding that reinforces the individual during periods of intense suffering.

High Desert

A Journey of Survival and Hope
KIM DOUGLAS
$20.00 U.S. / $22.00 CAN
Trade Paper
ISBN 978-1-931847-59-9

A deeply moving memoir with a holistic approach to overcoming the effects of growing up in a severely abusive home

High Desert is a courageous, gripping, and deeply personal autobiographical account about growing up in an abusive home and finding a path to recovery by learning to rely on faith and spiritual beliefs to heal and grow in ways that go beyond traditional twelve-step programs and other approaches. In this eye-opening account, Kim Douglas reveals a wide range of issues and behaviors that will be familiar to many who have come from similar circumstances: eating disorders, obsessive or compulsive behaviors, and troubled relationships with friends and family members. Most important is the author's insight and experience in finding effective ways of coping with life's challenges, learning to trust others in a close relationship, parenting without repeating the cycle of abuse, healing the relationship with the abuser, and forgiving those who don't help in a time of crisis.

Life at First Sight

Finding the Divine in the Details
PHYLLIS EDGERLY RING
$15.00 U.S. / $17.00 CAN
Trade Paper
ISBN 978-1-931847-67-4

Phyllis Ring divulges in this collection of personal essays how to "see the spiritual" in everyday moments and everyday life. Like love at first sight, "life at first sight" focuses on instant recognition and irresistible attraction, a sense of something mysteriously familiar and a sense of spiritual connection. The essays show how to develop a new sense of being during daily activities and everyday interactions, as well as through engagement with the natural world. As a jumping-off point for spiritual conversation, these compositions offer food for thought on how to lead a more spiritual life.

". . . Captures the web of meaning that unites and sustains all of human life. These sparkling essays remind us that the spiritual side of life is not a luxury or an optional nicety, but utterly crucial. At this moment in history, no message is more vital."—**Larry Dossey, MD, Author of** *The Power of Premonitions* **and** *The Extraordinary Healing Power of Ordinary Things*

"These essays are a treasure, especially as they pursue the journey of the human spirit through the perils—and joys—of 'the road not taken.' This is the sort of book that will warm, celebrate, and console the reader on a sour day. The book is lovingly written and beautifully conceived, and dares to approach the practical reality of the spiritual life."—**Dolores Kendrick, Poet Laureate of the District of Columbia and Author of** *Why the Woman Is Singing on the Corner* **and** *Now Is the Thing to Praise.*

The Universe Within Us

A Guide to the Purpose of Life
JANE E. HARPER
$15.00 U.S. / $17.00 CAN
Trade Paper
ISBN 978-1-931847-58-2

A provocative look at the purpose of life through a mixture of religion, science, and personal experience

Author Jane E. Harper offers insight into a new way to look at life. *The Universe Within Us* is a mixture of science, religion, and personal experience that offers a new understanding of our place and purpose in the universe—an understanding that leads to the conclusion that every human being possesses a spiritual nature. Harper argues that, traditionally, answers to questions about the purpose of life have long been the domain of priests and clergy, and, more recently, scientists—and often the answers have been less than satisfying. The religious answers often leave the intellect out and defy what the rational mind can accept, while the scientific answers satisfy the intellect at the expense of the heart and soul. Drawing on resources available from the sciences, from the world's sacred scriptures, and from personal observations and experiences, she offers a unique map of the universe and an explanation of life's purpose that is truly satisfying.